A Different Truth

Reject the Truths That Are Killing Your Career, and Learn to Make Choices That Are Better for You

JOANNA DENTON

ISBNs:
Hardcover 978-1-64184-154-2
Paperback 978-1-64184-155-9
ebook 978-1-64184-156-6

For Peter, whose death reminded me it was time to live.

CONTENTS

You can be the most successful leader, but if you are exhausted and running yourself into the ground, you will be no good to anyone. The problem is that often we believe we have to choose—our careers or our health. It's time to breathe a little and get back some headspace, and I will show you how to have both your career and your health.

Life's too short for you to stay small. It's time to step out of your comfort zone and step into your awesomeness. The only problem is, when you dream bigger and step up, those niggling self-doubts and criticisms come thick and fast and tell us we are not good enough. I will share three ways to rewire out of the fear into the possibility and manage your doubts so that they don't manage you.

How many times have you ever felt that you were on your own in this journey through life? There are people around you, but do they really get you? Do they really understand what your life is like? Do they really have any idea? What if that were not the case? Oh, to be celebrated for who you are and not merely tolerated for what you do! To be in a community that is there for you on the tough days and cheers you on the good ones, particularly as you start your journey toward dreaming bigger and stepping up. I will give you some exercises to build a community that encourages and empowers its members.

If you have gotten this far in your leadership journey based on technical genius alone and want to reach the next level, you have to tell your story to people outside your immediate community. But often we are brought up to believe that to do so would be far too aggressive and in your face. Here, I will give you three exercises to help you share your story in the wider marketplace without coming across as boastful or aggressive.

You are passionate about your subject. Hell's teeth, you wouldn't be doing what you are doing after all these years if that weren't the case. But it's easy to forget that mere mortals don't always understand what you are talking about, and equally easy to think they never will. I will give you three ways to connect with your audience without losing them in the technical weeds.

TRUTH

I t's 5 a.m.

5 a.m. on my thirty-fifth birthday and I just got home from work.

For the last couple of months, I have been working on a project with a West Coast client, and for the last couple of hours, I have been finishing some documents to send to them.

But now, everything is done and dusted, and I have come home.

It's been a particularly long week, and I must admit that 5 a.m. finishes are very unusual. I must also say that it feels like years that I have been working twelve to fourteen-hour days. And you know what? I am tired.

It's 5 a.m.

I should be sleeping, but instead I'm on the phone with my ex-boyfriend, and I am opening the present my parents have sent me. It's a framed picture of me and my sister from when I was fifteen years old.

Fifteen years old and my entire life ahead of me.

And at that moment, looking at the photo, I realise it.

The sum of my life is work.

I am a lawyer by training, and by now, I am nearly ten years into my career as tax consultant for an international accounting firm

On the face of it, I am some definition of success; I am the go-to person for my teams, my clients, and my bosses. I am someone who can come up with innovative solutions to very tricky problems, and I am also a role model for other women on my team.

But behind that definition of success is a pretty lonely existence. One of working long hours, nights, weekends, and holidays.

And slowly, my life is starting to fall apart. Always having to be the strong one, never asking for help.

I am just so tired of it all.

In that moment, looking at that picture, I realise that I don't want my life to be like this anymore. There has got to be more to life than this. And I am right, of course I am. There has to be.

But here's the problem.

I feel trapped.

Intellectually, I know there has got to be more to life than this, but emotionally, viscerally, in every other way of my being, I also believe that this exhaustion is the price you pay if you want to succeed in corporate life.

Because to work in corporate life, if I want to succeed and excel, means putting the hours in, sacrificing my personal life, and always being in competition. I learned that when I was young, and its been reinforced all through my life.

If I want to succeed in the corporate world, I have to choose work because I sure as hell can't choose life.

Because if I were to choose life—in other words to rest, take time to breathe, look after myself—I would be committing the cardinal sins of being selfish, lazy, and unprofessional. And worse still, if I were to ask for help, that would mean I was weak.

So, in that moment of realization, I don't have a choice. This is all there is. Work.

And the very next day, the day after my thirty-fifth birthday I get out of bed and I continue to do what I have always done.

I choose work.

Not to rest. Not to look after myself.

Work.

Because I believe I don't have a choice.

* * *

In the years that followed my thirty-fifth birthday, I kept on working to the same rhythm because I didn't know how to do anything else.

3

I didn't know how to slow down or breathe or take time for me. I just knew how to work. And so I did, and I kept on working till I burnt myself out.

Not once. But twice.

Until one day in 2014, six years after the photograph incident, when something happened that made me challenge the truth and change my choices.

By early 2014, I felt like I was constantly walking through molasses in a world where all the joy and colour had been sucked dry. I woke every morning filled with fear and dread—fear about going to a job that I no longer enjoyed and dread that others would see through this façade of success to see what I saw—that I was an imposter, bad at my job, and good for nothing.

It was burnout number two, and I was super-glued to the sofa.

Didn't want to wash, to eat, to go out.

And I sure as hell didn't want to tell anyone.

But on 6 March 2014, I had my life-changing wake-up call.

Not some gentle nudge from the universe like that twenty-year-old photo, or the panic attacks, or the OCD behaviours, or the trips to the emergency room with chest pains that I had had since my thirty-fifth birthday. No, it was a real, in-your-face wallop that I had no choice but to listen to.

That was the day of the funeral of a colleague, Peter.

At the age of sixty-seven, Peter had died suddenly, and I just had to be at the funeral. He was a gentleman, and a gentle man, and I needed to be there even if it meant leaving the apartment for the first time in weeks.

During the ceremony, I realised something. Peter hadn't just died of a heart attack. He had committed suicide.

He had spent the Saturday and Sunday with friends, laughing and joking. And the Monday morning he got up, he went to the red bridge in Luxembourg, and he jumped.

What stood out in particular during the service were the words of his friends.

"We would have been there in a moment," they said. "Why didn't he just tell us?"

Their sadness is clear—and also their confusion. They had spent time with him less than forty-eight hours before. But it was nobody's fault. Peter didn't want them to see what he was living. And so, he had not said a word.

As I got into the car that afternoon to come home, the tears came, and my heart broke.

At the age of sixty-seven, Peter believed that he didn't have a choice. He was living his own kind of hell, but he believed he couldn't tell anyone or reach out for help.

So, he did the only thing he could. He jumped.

As I sat in my car, I realised that there was something in his story that hit home and acted as a mirror for my own life. And for what my future might be if I continued to believe I had to do it all alone and not ask for help.

And I realised it didn't want that future.

And there was something in his story that gave me courage. Courage to make a different choice. Not to go home to an empty apartment and an empty sofa, but to pick up the phone, ask for help, and trust that someone would be there.

And so I did.

* * *

Over the last five years, I have picked myself up and taken back the power of my own choices. I have started to recognise and reject the stories that were ruling my life, and the truths that were killing my career. And I have started to make different choices.

But it took a lot of work.

At first, I needed to sleep, rest, and take some distance. I needed to find my friends again remember that I wasn't alone—and I needed to find a good therapist!

I started to see the stories I was telling myself about how life was meant to be. And I started to challenge those stories and ask myself if they were helping or hindering me.

When I was able to see those stories and start to unpack them, I was at last able to give myself permission to find a different truth about how life could be.

And in turn, that allowed me space to think long and hard about what it was I wanted or didn't want in my life. After sixteen years as a tax consultant, I finally decided that there was more to life than tax returns, and it was time to do something different.

Over the last five years, I have also realised that I am not alone in this adventure. I have spoken to other people about their experiences coming through a burnout to the other side.

What is clear from everyone is that they have all won a battle. They have all had to do the same work to unpack and examine their stories and start to deal with the shadows.

And they all have a day when they decided to choose themselves and their own well-being and to let go of the stories.

For one, it was a motorbike accident, or a colleague who dropped down dead at work. For another, it was the day she realised that she was so tired she couldn't remember how to make spaghetti Bolognese for her kids.

But whatever the trigger, one day there was a choice. And they made it.

* * *

And it is doing this work for myself, speaking to others who have also done it, and realising just how long we all took to learn these lessons that have inspired me to write this book.

Why should you have to wait until your world is falling apart to start to make different choices?

What if you could understand that you too have certain "truths" that you live by? What if you could allow yourself to challenge and change those truths? And allow that knowledge to help you make better choices?

And make them before it is too late.

That is my wish for you.

CHALLENGE

L et's talk about choices. The ones we make and the ones we don't make.

We make choices every day: big ones and small ones. And the choices we make define who we are and who we become.

Of course, we hope that all the choices we make are made freely. But often we are faced with situations where we tell ourselves we don't have a choice. There is no realistic option but a single course of action.

We believe that to be an absolute truth, but it is here that I have come to understand that this is just a story we tell ourselves.

Before going on, though, let me just make it clear what I am not talking about.

I am not talking about the low-income parents who have no choice but to work three jobs on minimum wage just to be able to put food on the table or someone in a burning building who has no choice but to get out of there.

What I am talking about is when you don't stand up to the bully because the bully is the boss, and you believe you don't have a choice. Or when you believe that you have to carry the load of all the work on your shoulders because you think no one else could do it as well as you and so you don't have a choice. Or when you stay in a shitty job that sucks away your soul and keeps you from your family because you believe you don't have a choice because you have to pay the mortgage for the big car, the big house, and the big holidays.

It's in those situations where I have come to learn that it's just a story. A story we tell ourselves. About how we don't have a choice.

And you know what. That's okay. That's human. Telling ourselves this kind of story is part of being human.

Because, of course, the story comes from somewhere. It comes from the rules that we have about how we need to live our lives. Rules that become the "truth."

They are rules that we learned as kids from our parents and our teachers, and they are rules that are reinforced through our own life experience.

Often, those rules propel us forward. They keep us safe and lead us toward the best form of ourselves.

But many don't. They lead us instead into pain and regret.

Maybe it's the rule that to serve others means to sacrifice our own wellbeing. Maybe it's the rule that we have to do it all alone and never ask for help. Or maybe it's the rule that the only way to truly measure happiness is with the big car, the big house, the big holiday.

But whatever the rule, whatever the story, over time, it gets so reinforced in our mind that it becomes the "truth." The truth about how life is.

About how we don't have a choice.

And faced with that "truth," we don't choose.

But here's the thing—the fact of not choosing is a choice in itself. And when we choose one thing, we don't choose something else.

All of our choices have consequences. The ones we make; and the ones we don't make.

Sometimes, the choices we don't make are the ones that have the biggest consequences.

As an example, some of my truths, such as the ones about success equalling long hours of work or about how if life is easy, you're not doing it right, led me down a path of more and more work and longer and longer hours. A path of choosing work and not choosing my own well-being. I eventually burnt out—twice. When that happened, I had to make a choice. Either I could change and take control of my life, or I could let my stories, my beliefs, my truth run me, and my life, into the ground. I thought my truth would make my career, but it killed it. I ran out of the health or strength needed to continue it in the same way.

But that's just one way our truths can affect us and kill our careers. Some truths will lead to ill health. Others, perhaps ones you don't even know you're telling yourself, lead to different destinations: insecurity, fear, stagnation, sadness, isolation, et cetera. These truths can keep you from reaching out for the next promotion or project, isolate you from the community you desperately need, and silence you because no one understands what you are saying, if you're saying anything at all.

This book aims to help you notice those truths and where they lead so that you can challenge and change them.

It might not be easy. When I was 35, I didn't know I was following a narrative; I was just doing my best to lead a successful life. I was living what I believed to be the truth.

But it left me completely drained and with only work to show for it. My colleague's death jolted me out of that exhausted stupour and caused me to start examining what I believed about work, life, and myself. Eventually, I took steps—made choices—to change the narratives that were running my life.

That's what the rest of this book is about. Besides noticing and challenging career-killing narratives and truths, we'll cover how to take a different choice and step into healthy, life-giving truths.

* * *

Quick check in and reality check here—is all of that really so easy? Is it easy to let go of that truth and find a different one? To make a different choice?

Of course it's not easy, and here's why.

It's not easy because often we don't even see that it's a story, we just see it to be the "truth".

It's not easy because sometimes if we do think there is a choice, there is a deep-rooted guilt that comes floating to the surface at the prospect of doing something different. And it can be this guilt that is the most difficult thing to shift.

And it's not easy because, if we are truly honest, to take a decision to do something different is to admit we're in control of our own destiny. And it's giving up the possibility to live our lives as a victim of everyone else and of the world.

So of course it's not easy.

But it can be done.

You can make a different choice. And choose a different story.

But it starts with noticing the story in the first place.

First, notice what the voice is saying to you and look for the story behind. Here, for example, notice when the voice tells you that you don't have a choice, and find the story behind the statement. For example, for me, I was telling myself that to slow down meant I was lazy; if I was lazy, I would never succeed or be excellent.

Be kind to yourself and accept that this story has been there for a long time.

Second, question the story. Is it helping or hindering you? Flash-forward five or ten years—if you kept that narrative, what impact would it have on your life, your health, your well-being?

Third, change the story. What would be a more helpful narrative? For example, for me, I now tell myself that if I rest when my body needs it, I can come back even stronger and be able to serve my clients and my tribe even better.

In this book, I invite you to take that leap of faith, a leap of faith to see that there is a story there somewhere. I am going to shine a light on some of those stories in particular.

And I am going to give you exercises to move through that story to a different choice …

Let's consider an example. In the chapter "Connect," I start with a narrative we sometimes tell ourselves: "My technical subject is so difficult and boring that no one will ever understand it, so why should I bother trying?"

If we believe that that truth is just the way life is, we won't even bother trying to make the subject interesting for our audience. We will deliver our talk and wonder why we're peering into a sea of bemused faces.

On the other hand, when our charismatic colleague gets on stage, the dynamic shifts. The audience leans forward rather than peers at their cell phones. We might feel a little irate; our colleague is blowing a bunch of hot air, but what can we do about it? He's connected with the audience in a way we don't think we can. He's the fun speaker, and we, by comparison, are the well-informed but stodgy one.

Fortunately, we don't have to continue in the trajectory of that belief. We can change it, make the subject interesting, and capture our audience's ears and minds.

But how? Well, that's what this book is for. I've pulled together a bunch of things I have come across, used, and digested over the years—things that have helped me on my own journey—and I have done so with the hope that they will help you not only consider other narratives but also practice them. So, for example, in the case of connecting with your audience, we'll walk through three ways to better communicate your subject, technical or otherwise, with your listeners.

The other chapters work similarly. To give you an idea of what's in store, check out these brief chapter descriptions.

1. Thrive

You can be the most successful leader, but if you are exhausted and running yourself into the ground, you will be no good to anyone. The problem is that often we believe we have to choose—our careers or our health. It's time to breathe a little and get back some headspace, and I will show you how to have both your career and your health.

2. Rewire

Life's too short for you to stay small. It's time to step out of your comfort zone and step into your awesomeness. The only problem is, when you dream bigger and step up, those niggling self-doubts and criticisms come thick and fast and tell us we are not good enough. I will share three ways to rewire out of the fear into the possibility and manage your doubts so that they don't manage you.

3. Community

How many times have you ever felt that you were on your own in this journey through life? There are people around you, but do they really get you? Do they really understand what your life is like? Do they really have any idea? What if that were not the case? Oh, to be celebrated for who you are and not merely tolerated for what you do! To be in a community that is there for you on the tough days and cheers you on the good ones, particularly as you start your journey toward dreaming bigger and stepping up. I will give you some exercises to build a community that encourages and empowers its members.

4. Story

If you have gotten this far in your leadership journey based on technical genius alone and want to reach the next level, you have to tell your story to people outside your immediate community. But often we are brought up to believe that to do so would be far too aggressive and in your face. Here, I will give you three exercises to help you share your story in the wider marketplace without coming across as boastful or aggressive.

5. Connect

You are passionate about your subject. Hell's teeth, you wouldn't be doing what you are doing after all these years if that weren't the case. But it's easy to forget that mere mortals don't always understand what you are talking about, and equally easy to think they never will. I will give you three ways to connect with your audience without losing them in the technical weeds.

In each chapter, we will explore a new truth through:

- Personal stories and example narratives

- Appreciative enquiry exercise to help you identify your strengths and goals

- A five-minute exercise to move you forward today

- Three in-depth exercises to build long-lasting, positive change

TOOLS

Each of the chapters ask you to use the following three tools:

- Journaling

  Journaling puts pen to paper and records your thoughts in response to prompts. If you don't know what to write, start there. "I don't know what to write because I've never had to think about [fill in the blank] before." The pen, and your mind, will find its way toward filling in that blank.

- Real Play, Not Role Play

  As you work through the chapters' exercises, think about real situations, not hypotheticals. I want you to walk away with practical steps you can apply to your life now, not act out a role.

- Progress, Not Perfection

  The exercises want you to take an action and move forward, but the action doesn't need to be perfect. Just act! The important thing is to keep stepping forward no matter how imperfectly.

GETTING STARTED

It's up to you how to work through this book. You could walk through it on your own and see how the exercises help you move forward.

You might find the book more effective if you work through the book with a couple of good friends or work colleagues. Spend time reflecting on the work on your own but gather together for a monthly debrief session. There, talk about what you've learned and the steps you are putting in place.

And look, if you find that things are coming up for you that you want to work on further with proper professional support, do like I did and find a good coach or therapist (or both) to work with. It goes without saying that no book can be or is ever meant to be a substitute for that.

In terms of *where* to start in the book, you could open to any chapter and find a practical exercise designed to shift things in a tangible, positive way. But you may prefer something more linear. If so, read through the book as you would any other, beginning to end. The book is designed to meet you where you're at and help you take the next step, whether that's one step or a series of them.

It's your turn, now. Breathe, and then make a choice to examine your narratives, challenge the ones that need to be challenged, and step into new narratives that lead where you want to go.

THRIVE

In 2014, I decided to reorient my career in tax and make coaching people on public speaking an integral part of my job. I made that choice because I'd had two burnouts in five years, and when the second one happened, I finally realised there was more to life than tax returns.[1] It was time to live life itself.

And that meant changing my life. It was either that or risk having a heart attack before I turned 45.

But people don't always get how it took a *second* burnout to realize that about myself.

Their astonishment seems to imply, "How could you be so stupid as to put yourself back into the same state as before? Surely you must have learned all this before?"

The thing is, I'd been systematically running myself into the proverbial brick wall and then getting up and getting on with it since I was 16. It was a normal state for me.

But that didn't make it healthy. When my second burnout happened, I realised I needed to get my shit in gear and make a fundamental shift in mind-set. I had to give myself permission to look after myself. If I didn't, I would continue to work like a mad thing, thinking I had to do it all by myself and convincing myself that asking for help was a sign of weakness.

Great idea, but there was a problem: I didn't think it was acceptable to look after myself. I thought it meant I was lazy.

Okay, that statement probably sounds twisted. It is.

Let's break down what was going through my head to figure out how I got to where I was.

- I believed surviving in my chosen career meant I needed to be excellent in, and fully committed to, everything I did.[2]

---

1. A controversial statement, I must admit.

2. Just to be clear, I still believe I need to be committed and excellent in what I do. However, the way I manifest and live out those principles has shifted.

- I believed excellence and commitment were demonstrated by, and directly proportional to, the number of hours I worked.

- I believed, therefore, a choice had to be made: I could either be excellent and committed by working the hours (even if they made me ill). OR, I could look after myself and not work the hours, but if I did, people (peers, bosses, clients) would no longer perceive me as excellent and committed.

As I sit here writing this, I find myself asking, "Is there any logic to this argument?" The answer, with hindsight, screams, "Hell, no!!"

But at the time, and at the moment, it seemed like the most logical thought in the world[3].

You may have followed a similar pattern of thinking, especially if you have worked in a corporate environment at some point in your career or were the over-achieving student.

The idea isn't odd. We are taught—at school, in uni, in life—that you put in the hours and work hard to get the best grades. If you get the best grades, you get the best jobs and opportunities. Once you get the job, you work harder and put in even more hours to get the promotion and rise to the next level. Then, you continue working hard to get the pay increase, the title, and so on and so on, until you retire. Only then can you start to enjoy things.

We are taught to sacrifice. To sacrifice ourselves, our health, and our happiness in the pursuit of success.

---

3. Let me be clear about something at this point: Excellence and time spent have little to do with each other. I once thought excellence was demonstrated by long hours at work. However, long hours have little to do with excellence. It's quite the opposite, really. For me, long hours often meant crappy decisions. I was too tired to think. Many times, I'd draft a memo or email in a trance-like state, return to it later, and not recognise a single word on the page.

At the very least, these thoughts were true for me. I learnt the lessons and lived by them when I went into corporate life in the 1990s. Before I knew it, five, ten, fifteen years had passed, and I was well and truly brainwashed into the "work hard, work long hours" frame of mind. I had put so many hours into my work that I considered my way of life to be the right way of life, so much so that I expected everyone else to follow suit.

Intellectually I might have been the first to extol the virtues of balance. But emotionally, physically, and in every other way, I had a problem with team members who wanted to work from 9 to 5. Ironically, I became part of the problem for a new generation working with and for me.

And ultimately, I hit a brick wall—several of them, in fact. A brick wall full of exhaustion, panic attacks, and obsessive-compulsive behaviour. Some days it would take me ten minutes to leave work because I would go back and forth, in and out of the office, making sure I hadn't dropped anything. I had panic attacks leaving my car at the airport to go on business trips, so I started to pay for cabs to take me there, fly the night before, and pay for my own hotel room to stay over. And I had entire checklists to complete before leaving my apartment.

Life was bloody miserable.

Until I stopped and took stock. When I did, I made significant choices about what was *really* important to me and how I would live my life.

I changed, and things changed. They had to if I wanted to survive until my forty-fifth birthday. In doing so, I learned a mighty lesson: I didn't need to choose between career and health. If I wanted to excel in either one, I needed to thrive in both.

So do you, so please listen. **You don't have to choose between your career and your health.** You can have both.

THRIVING MEANS LOOKING AFTER YOURSELF

To thrive you have got to look after yourself. And that means giving yourself permission to be human, imperfect, and know that that is enough.

Thriving, though, requires a few things besides permission. It also involves understanding—actually, not just understanding, but belief—that you don't have to kill yourself with work to be successful.

Thriving takes one more element: Doing one thing, every day, to breathe and fill yourself with energy. It may sound like an absurd idea, but if you think about it in the cold light of day, it's pretty bonkers to wait all year for your three-week holiday simply to take time for yourself.[4]

Now, I do get it. The idea of doing something every day to take time for yourself can seem unfathomable when you work *all* the time.[5] But if you maintain that pace, you'll run yourself into a wall. All the things you have been fighting for, the game-changing ideas you have, will be for nothing. You'll

---

4. Particularly when chances are you will spend the first week asleep recovering from the late nights of work getting ready to go on holiday; the middle week fretting about the emails that are coming in because the team seems incapable of surviving without you; and the last week getting stressed out about going back to work and all the stuff you will need to do to make up for your three weeks off.

5. And let's not forget those of you who are also running around after families over and above your working hours.

make yourself ill or get to the end of the course you've set yourself upon and realise no one is there to watch you succeed. You lost them somewhere in your pursuit of succeeding at the expense of thriving.

If you choose the other course, you will look after yourself. You'll feel rested because you're slowing down and taking time to make decisions; you aren't rushing from one thing to the next.

Instead, you're plotting a course, making time for deep and creative work. As you do, you gain a stronger ability to focus because your time isn't taken up with all the things. It's taken up with the best things.

Besides having time for things that matter, you'll have time for friends and family. You may even become an example, showing friends, family, and peers a positive way forward. They'll begin to see they don't have to choose career over health. They can have both.

As for burnout or getting sick, you'll minimise their risks. At the very least, you'll have acquired a sufficient distance from the busyness of life to recognise when the symptoms begin to develop. That recognition gives you power. You can change your course when the warning signs appear, ensuring you reach your desired destination.

EXAMINE WHERE YOU
ALREADY THRIVE

Before you jump into the exercises, let's figure out where you already thrive, the times and places where you already take care of yourself.

I'll help you discover that knowledge with an application of Appreciative Inquiry[6]. Once you understand how and why you already take care of yourself, you can leverage the knowledge to reach new heights in every area of your life.

Maybe you get your hair done every month and spend a couple of hours with gunk on your head at the hair salon. Or maybe it's Sunday brunch with friends or family catching up on all the news. Perhaps you simply rock out to Pharrell Williams' "Happy" in the car on the way to work or re-watch your favourite episode of James Corden's "Carpool Karaoke" or episodes of Graham Norton's TV show on YouTube.[7] Others choose other methods, things like meditation, a game of tennis, or yoga.[8]

---

6. Organisations use Appreciative Inquiry to identify and build upon strengths to bring about change. Individuals also use the methodology to effect change through a strengths-based approach. The assessment tool comes from creators David Cooperrider and Suresh Srivastva, and I will use this tool in all the chapters of the book before we start different exercises.

7. At the time of writing this, my top James Corden "Carpool Karaokes" are Broadway musicals, Adele, and Paul McCartney. My fave Graham Norton show must be either the one with Will.i.am, Miriam Margoyles and Greg Davis, or the episode with the cast of *Monuments Men*: Matt Damon, Hugh Bonneville, and Bill Murray.

8. Just to avoid any doubt, I am more of a chocolate and Graham Norton kind of girl.

The point is, thriving happens in those moments where you stop and take time to breathe. It is the moments where time stands still, and you walk away feeling energised and full of joy.

That's what I call a thriving state, and I hope you already experience it in some ways. I would like you to (a) find those existing moments and (b) leverage them to reach new heights.

Let's get started.

Step 1. Define what you want to achieve
In the context of taking care of yourself and thriving, what goal do you want to achieve? What mountains could you move, lives could you change, dreams could you realise, if you just gave yourself time to breathe?

Step 2. Discover your existing strengths
What activities make you feel valuable and alive? Where do you tend to thrive? How do you already thrive well?

Step 3. Dream about possibilities
Let your imagination run wild. What could happen if you were to prioritize your health and well-being? How might your example inspire others to do the same?

Step 4. Design your roadmap
Using the insights gained from the previous questions, what should your milestones be? How will you achieve your desired goal(s)?

Step 5. Deliver on destiny
What next steps will move you toward that ideal state?

You have chosen some first steps. That's fantastic. But you can do more to thrive, each and every day. The next few exercises will guide you through how to do that.

PRACTICE: WRITE YOURSELF A PERMISSION SLIP

I know you are busy. But this is important. **You have to look after yourself.**

"Okay, Joanna, I hear you, but how am I going to stop the world and get off this wildly circling planet for five minutes a day?"

Here's a starting point: Give yourself permission to at least try.

If you were to close your eyes and think of something you would really like to do for yourself, but don't do because you think it would be far too indulgent, what would it be?

Perhaps it's to leave the office at 5 p.m. for once and meet a friend for a drink. Perhaps it is to take a nice long bath, pig out on an Indian takeaway, or go get a massage. Or maybe it's not to know all the answers all the time and to be okay with that.

Whatever your "thing" is, it's time to write yourself a permission slip to do it. Give yourself permission to do whatever it is that you have been waiting for someone else to allow you to do. Think of it like the permission slip your mum might write for you at school to get you out of games class. And then carry it around with you so you can show it to others if they question your meal choices or leaving work at a decent hour.[9]

---

9. I love the idea of permission slips for this context. I first came across it in this context in Brene Brown's books. She talks about permission, too. Check her out here: https://youtu.be/NY6hZf6kI4g.

PRACTICE: THRIVE EVERY DAY

We all face a choice in life. Either we choose to let life drive our destiny, or we choose to be the drivers of our destiny.

I believe we—each and all of us—can select the second option. When we direct our destinies and take hold of our power, we experience more happiness and satisfaction. We probably sense those feelings, however vaguely, when we make choices that contribute to our growth. But research affirms our instincts. I'll share some of that information in the following exercises because it's important to know the *why* behind what we do. It gives us a foundation from which to speak and act when doubts arise, or people criticise.

And more importantly, I get it. You have built your life and career on the basis of hard facts, and the last thing anyone is likely to do is describe you as "whoo whoo" or new age. If I said to you, let's go out into nature and sit on the ground and tune into the inherent energy of the planet, you would probably run a mile in the other direction. But if I were to quote scientific research related to thriving, you would be more likely to listen and maybe even adopt some new practices.

Over the next pages we will:

- Write a love letter to ourselves to remember we are worth looking after.

- Find activities to do in five minutes every day that restore our energy and purpose.

- Choose to step into our truest and best selves.

WRITE YOURSELF A LOVE LETTER

It has taken several years and a lot of inner work for me to believe I am allowed to look after myself and am important enough to look after. And I *do* believe that. I am valuable and should treat myself as someone who is of infinite worth.

Because I am. And so are you. This is the undeniable truth: You—yes, you!—are someone special. And when I say special, I don't mean some random list of achievements. Those are *what* you do. By special, I mean *who* you are. You, my friend, are special. You're unique, too. There is only one of you. That means if you don't look after yourself, the world will lose the light that is *you*.

Maybe you already know you're special and valuable and unique. Fantastic! This first exercise ought to be easy because I'm going to ask you to articulate *why* you are amazing and worth looking after. For others, me included, this exercise can feel awkward and ridiculous, especially the first time around. But bear with me, because if you can complete this exercise, you will find yourself beginning to allow yourself to thrive in any situation and circumstance.

So, what's the exercise? I want you to write yourself a love letter.[10] NO, SERIOUSLY—write one!

---

10. I did warn you that the exercise would seem absurd at first glance.

If you're thinking, "Ew, gross," or "I can't do that," take a deep breath. We're going to work through three exercises and build up to the letter slowly. If that's not your style, feel free to jump to the end and pen yourself that love note.

1. Ask your friends what they see in you.

2. Write a birthday speech from the viewpoint of your child, best friend, or love of your life.

3. Write yourself a love letter, telling yourself why you love, appreciate, and are grateful for you.

EXERCISE #1. ASK YOUR FRIENDS WHAT THEY LOVE ABOUT YOU

Two questions.

1. Do you know what your closest friends see in you?

2. Have you ever asked them?

If you haven't, well, today's the day. I'm going to ask you to reach out to your friends and ask, "What's so great about me? Why are we friends?"

Now, there are some ground rules for this exercise.

First, by reaching out to friends, I mean contacting two, three, or five true friends. Friends you trust and respect, and friends you know will be honest with you. So, to avoid any doubt at all, I do not mean a post on Facebook or a mass email to your 1,000 LinkedIn contacts.

Second: Be upfront about what you're doing. Tell them you are doing self-exploration exercise and ask your questions.

1. "What do you see in me?"

2. "Why did you become my friend?"

3. "Why are you still my friend?"

Finally—wait. Just wait to see what they come back with.

I think you will be touched, moved, and surprised. I know I was when I did this exercise a few years ago.

When I asked some friends why they thought I was awesome, I was blown away by the sincerity and perspective in the responses. Of course they were sincere; they were only ever going to be sincere, which is why I chose to ask them and not others. But to see in black and white, and to read the wonderful things they thought about me, was inspiring and validating. Their kind words said they saw me for who I was and for the values I wanted to be known by. And it was incredible to know I was truly seen.

EXERCISE #2. WRITE YOUR BIRTHDAY SPEECH

Imagine the scene: It is your birthday. The room brims with balloons, chocolate cake, and your favouritest people in the world. The drinks flow, the waiters serve the yummiest food, and people buzz in celebration of you.

A clink-clink sounds, and your loved one[11] takes the mic. The room quiets, and as it does, your most-most-favourite person says:

Friends, family, everyone, thank you for being here. I am so happy to see so many of you—some from down the road, others from further afield—and all of you are here to celebrate this, the birthday of (INSERT YOUR NAME).

Now, we all know (INSERT YOUR NAME).

Although (INSERT YOUR NAME) is always running around doing things for all of us, and we all know

---

11. Son, daughter, spouse, partner, significant other, best friend, parent, sibling, etc, etc. Only you know which loved one would take centre stage to applaud the person who is you.

(s)he[12] doesn't really like being in the spotlight or talking about himself/herself.

So, (s)he's not going to speak tonight. I am. And I am going to tell you the truth—the truth you will never hear from him/her. I am going to tell you why this (wo)man is the most amazing person you will EVER, and I mean EVER, meet.

So, let me now tell you what makes (INSERT YOUR NAME) the most special and wonderful person I have ever known.

Now, continue the speech. Write down what your loved one would say if asked to give a birthday speech in your honour.

EXERCISE #3. WRITE THE LOVE LETTER

Okay, you have some great material, thanks to listening to others, which means it's time to write your letter.

Get yourself something yummy—a glass of wine, a cup of tea, or a lovely, warm bath, whatever it takes—and bring along some paper and a pen. It's time to write yourself a letter, a *love* letter to be exact.

This love letter is going to be from you to yourself. It will set out in black and white what it is you love and appreciate about yourself and why you deserve to be looked after and cared for.

If you aren't sure how to start yours, follow the example shown here.

---

12. He or she, you know what I mean. ☺

Dear (INSERT YOUR NAME),

Gawd, it's been ages since I last wrote to tell you how much I love you. Because, you know, I do, I BLOOM-ING ADORE YOU.

I know I sometimes take you for granted and don't look after you properly. Okay, okay, I ALWAYS take you for granted. I make you stay up late playing games on your iPad instead of going to bed, convince you to eat chocolate biscuits rather than fruit and yogurt for breakfast, and refuse to get out of bed in the morning to take you to yoga.

IT DOESN'T MEAN I DON'T LOVE YOU, YOU EEJIT.[13]

But I wouldn't be surprised if you had forgotten that because I don't always properly tell you you're loved.

I am going to correct that and tell you how much you're loved right now.

You rock my world because…

I appreciate you because…

I am grateful to you because…

And you know what? It's about time I showed you that I love you, too. So, this is what I am going to do for you, (INSERT YOUR NAME), to show how much I care.

I am going to do…for you because…

And I am going to do that starting now.

Lots of love, cuddles and chocolate cake (with a bit of fruit for breakfast, too),

(INSERT YOUR NAME)

Take as long as it takes to write your letter but do write it in one sitting. If you leave in the middle of writing it, you may never return or have to start the writing process all over

---

13. Eejit: A Northern Irish word for "idiot."

again. Once written, seal the letter in a self-addressed envelope and ask someone to post it back to you. One day it'll arrive in your post-box out of the blue.

How did that feel? What are you thinking now that you've taken some time to remember you are worth looking after?

I hope the exercise convinced you of the need for a new narrative when it comes to caring about your physical, emotional, and spiritual health.

If it did, great! The next exercise introduces some different activities designed to support your new narrative and improve overall happiness and well-being.

TAKE TIME TO BREATHE, EVERY SINGLE DAY

Over the years research studies have been undertaken to determine how different factors impact our levels of happiness and overall life satisfaction. In particular, researchers have looked at the influence of genetics (or the notion of a happiness setpoint), of external events or circumstances, and of intentional activities.[i] The study suggests that while there is an element of overlap between all factors and as such they cannot be seen as completely independent, intentional activities—the things we consciously think, do, or feel—have a sizeable influence on our overall level of happiness.

Whichever way you look at it, that has to be good news to reinforce the notion that we are the driver of our destiny. We can do things to take care of ourselves and improve our sense of life satisfaction, even in the moments when we feel that someone else is driving the car that is our life.

Now, we could do a bunch of big stuff and completely overhaul our lives from one day to the next, but you and I both know that that is neither realistic nor sustainable. So, I do want to focus on something a lot more manageable and natural: **small things** we can do on a regular basis. These are activities we may already enjoy doing or could easily integrate into our daily rhythms.

Let's look at some examples of what I mean. In her book *The How of Happiness,* Sonja Lyubomirsky identifies twelve research-based activities that can build happiness. These are as follows:

1. Express gratitude

2. Cultivate optimism

3. Avoid overthinking and social comparison

4. Perform acts of kindness

5. Nurture relationships

6. Develop coping strategies

7. Learn to forgive

8. Engage in flow

9. Savour life's joys

10. Commit to your goals

11. Practice religion and spirituality

12. Take care of your body

I don't profess to be any kind of expert in this field, but I have had fun reading about these activities to find out what works for me. In the pages that follow, I will take you through each and give you some additional links to other articles.

I could, of course, just tell you to go out and do all of the above. But let's not do that. First, such advice is scary. Second, it's impractical. Not everything works for everybody. We each have preferences about what feels more or less natural to do. And third, we want appealing activities we'll enjoy, not ones that become incredibly tedious.

So, I'm going to suggest two options.

Option 1: Find Your Best Fit
The activity that gives the maximum outcome for your efforts is going to be the one that matches your interests, values, and needs the most.

In order to find this, you can access an online questionnaire[14] developed by Sonja Lyubomirsky.

This questionnaire will ask you to return to the list of twelve activities, and to reflect on them, thinking about:

- Ease. If you started the activity, would it be easy to start and stick with?

- Interest. Do you find the activity interesting or potentially enjoyable?

- Value. Do you value the activity for the sake of the activity? Do you identify with it in some way?

- Guilt. If you don't follow through with the activity, will you feel guilty?

- Pressure. Are you choosing an activity because someone said you should?[15]

Once you evaluate the suggested activities on the above criteria, choose your top two or three. Then, continue to the descriptions of the different activities to see why they work and how they can be used in day-to-day life.

---

14. Take Lyubomirsky's questionnaire at https://pathtohappier.com.

15. Be careful here. A counsellor's or doctor's advice is different from that of a friend saying you have to try a new fad diet or exercise regimen. If your doctor is telling you to do it, you should probably follow their advice.

Option 2: Start with an Activity

Maybe you want to get to work on thriving. If so, continue on. Read the activities' descriptions and start with the ones that seem most helpful to where you are now and where you want to go next.

1. EXPRESS GRATITUDE

A 2016 study about gratitude and conducted by Charlotte van Oyen Witvliet, Fallon J. Richie, Lindsey M. Root Luna, and Daryl R. Van Tongeren made an interesting discovery: Gratitude was a predictor of hope and happiness.[ii] Why? Pausing for a moment or three causes you to notice the good things already happening in your life and the lives of others.[iii][16]

Example Activities

- Keep a gratitude journal. Once a week[17], write down two or three things you are grateful for that day. Include how you contributed to those things in your writings[18].

- Writing your daily things on a sticky note before bed. Stick it on either your bedside lamp or bathroom mirror so it greets you first thing in the morning.

- Write a thank-you note. Think of someone you wish to thank for something truly life changing, but whom you

---

16. For additional research about gratitude, check out Gratefulness.org.

17. The debate on how often to do this practice is quite interesting. While the starting point was usually every day, other researchers recognised that writing in a gratitude journal daily could become more about ticking boxes than a truly intentional practice.

18. The idea is to add how you contributed to the positive thing you are grateful for and to reinforce and anchor the idea that you are the captain of your ship. You are not simply a beneficiary of "luck."

have never before thanked. Write them a letter and either deliver it in person or through the mail.

2. CULTIVATE OPTIMISM

In "Optimism and Its Impact on Mental and Physical Well-Being," researchers Ciro Conversano and others say optimism can directly influence your mental and physical health. The effects occur because optimism is both a style of thinking and a hopeful outlook on the world. Because of it, you're more likely to develop a healthy lifestyle and positive coping strategies, leading to "greater flexibility and problem-solving capacity."[iv]

Considering those outcomes, we should all exercise optimism. It helps regain control of our life and enhances performance at work, home, and everywhere else.

Example Activities

- Visualise your future, happy self and create a vision board to represent that future self. Gather together old magazines and picture books, then use images from them to create a vision board of what life could be like five years from now if every day were to go as well as it possibly could. When you have created the vision board, look at the different elements on there, and recognise which relate to the realisation of your dreams and goals that you have today. This can help you identify your most important and meaningful aspirations, which can in turn help you feel more hopeful.

- -Channel your energy. How we think often shapes our perceptions and responses. When you start having negative thoughts, channel them to the "sunnier side of things."[19] This action can be hard, especially if you gravitate toward pessimism, but it can be helpful. Think of the activity as being realistic about all the possible outcomes, negative and positive, and try to direct your thoughts and energy toward the positive ones.

- Redefine optimism. We sometimes think optimism equals happiness. But that isn't necessarily the case. Optimism is about "approaching hardship in a more productive way," says Kimberly Hershenson, LMSW.[v] Instead of blaming yourself for everything, you view setbacks as temporary and plan to experience positive events in the future.

3. AVOID OVERTHINKING AND SOCIAL COMPARISON

Comparing ourselves to others is engrained in our psyche.[vi] We compare ourselves when we collaborate and when we compete.

The first has the potential to make us feel better about ourselves when we stand beside peers and equals to take on the world and kick some serious ass—but only if our collaborators are better than us. If the collaborator is worse, we might also start to feel incompetent.

And when we're competing, the comparison shifts. A skilled competitor against us makes us feel our performance is worse; an unskilled one makes us feel our performance is better.

What does all that mean? How we judge ourselves owes a lot to how and how often we think of others. Unfortunately,

---

19. I'm not saying you have to turn yourself into a happy-go-lucky person who has no care in the world because they no longer have a grasp on reality, but there might be ways to be a little more positive. For example, it might come down to vocabulary. Instead of thinking, "I never get this right," think, "Is it really never? Or is it rarely?" Be specific when you answer the question so you can identify when and where you get it right.

we often get stuck comparing ourselves to others rather than celebrating who we and they are.

Example Activities

- Make a list of things you have achieved. Now, really savour them by having a small celebration. What would a celebration look like for you? Is that a bar of chocolate? A luxurious bath? A night out with friends? What ever form that celebration might take, do it in full mindfulness of what you want to celebrate. When you can do that, you'll find yourself looking less at the "competition" and more at what you have achieved and been given.

- Find a new way to measure success. If we base success on a comparison of self to others, we'll never gain steady footing. We'll constantly look over our shoulders and spend every waking moment trying to outperform a colleague or neighbour. Let's define success in a way that's unique to who we are and what we want to do.

- Focus on your life. Joshua Becker at *Becoming Minimalist* says, "You can control one life—yours."[vii] So own it. Don't waste time and energy peering into other people's lives. What you see on their outsides cannot be compared to your insides.

4. PERFORM ACTS OF KINDNESS

When you get stuck in a negative stage, you may close yourself off to other people's joys and pains. Kindness, giving or doing something without expecting anything in return, can improve your mood, set you on a spiral upward, and increase your overall wellbeing.[viii] Remember, too, that your act of kindness often inspires others to follow your example.[ix]

Example Activities

- Pay for a cup of coffee for the person in line behind you.

- Buy a meal for a homeless person.

- Offer help. Think of a person at work or in your neighbourhood who could use help with a task. Now, offer assistance.

5. NURTURE RELATIONSHIPS

The Mental Health Foundation offers extensive research on relationships. The organization says "good-quality relationships can help us to live longer and happier lives with fewer mental health problems. Having close, positive relationship can give us a sense of purpose and sense of belonging."[x]

Example Activities

- Reconnect with friends and family. Contact someone you haven't been in touch with for a while and with whom you want to reconnect. Go for lunch or coffee to catch up properly.

- Form a mentoring relationship and establish a routine for getting together on a regular basis.

- Listen—really listen. Don't just listen to know the next question you want to ask.[20] Listen to really understand what the person is saying and feeling.

---

20. ...which isn't really listening anyway. There are different levels of listening, and the deepest requires setting yourself aside, giving the other person the floor, and listening not only with your ears but also your soul.

6. DEVELOP COPING STRATEGIES

Relationships and optimistic outlooks are two examples of coping strategies. Coping strategies are there to help us handle difficult or stressful situations. When we encounter difficulties, we turn to a trusted friend or take a deep breath before returning to the fray. But we can develop other coping strategies, too.

Example Activities

- Journal about what you're experiencing. Whether you've had a quality day or suffered a huge setback or upset at work, write about it.

- Move your body. Refocus your mind's attention by getting some exercise. Practice yoga, go for a run, swim some laps, or take a boxing class—you choose.

- Meet with your most trusted allies. Sometimes, you just need to vent. Find your allies, close the door, and talk about all hell breaking loose. Check out the part of the book on Community for more on this.

7. LEARN TO FORGIVE

You may never forget how that person hurt you, but by forgiving them, you let go of the hurt and anger. And as such, forgiveness becomes a gift you give yourself. You forgive the person and let go of the hurt and anger so that you can move forward with your life.

Forgiveness also produces physical benefits. It can lower your blood pressure, lessen the symptoms of depression, and improve heart health.[xi] Forgiveness is good for your mind, body, and soul.

Example Activities

- Think about when you received forgiveness. Before you are able to forgive someone else, you may need to remember how much you have been forgiven. What insights does that memory give? How easy was it to ask forgiveness? How easy was it for that person to show you forgiveness?

- Ask yourself how it helps you to hold on to the anger you feel toward a particular person. Does it really help you? What if you could forgive them? Imagine that forgiveness. Imagine forgiving the person who hurt you, even if you never speak with them again. What does forgiveness look like? Feel like?

- Sometimes the person we need to forgive is no longer around for us to forgive them. If this is the case, sit down and write them a letter setting out what you would want to say to them if they were around. Sometimes writing those thoughts down can be as powerful as saying them out loud to the person.

8. ENGAGE IN FLOW

Mihaly Csikszentmihalyi, in his book *Flow*, defines flow as "a state in which people are so involved in an activity that nothing else seems to matter; the experience is so enjoyable that people will continue to do it even at great cost, for the sheer sake of doing it."[xii]

He expands on the concept with eight characteristics: intense absorption, clarity of goals, transformation of time, intrinsically rewarding experiences, effortlessness, an appropriate balance of challenge and skills, merged awareness and action, and sense of control.

You may not recognize all those qualities while in a flow state. But if you've ever lost track of time when working on a meaningful project, you can more-or-less bet you've been "in the flow." You'll want to get to that frame of mind again because flow states cause creativity and well-being to flourish.

Example Activities

You will know the activities that make your heart sing and in which you can lose yourself completely. The following exercises are designed to simply give you the bandwidth and head-space to give yourself to them.

- Get rid of mental clutter. Spend half an hour brain-dumping your to-do list on to a page—you know, all those things that keep swimming around in your head. Look at that to-do list and remove anything that has been "pending" for the last couple of months. Let's face it, if you haven't done it yet, you will probably never get around to it. For the rest, give each item on it both a priority and set amount of time. Defining the order you'll do things in can prevent tasks from intruding upon your flow.

- Remove physical clutter. Having lots of "stuff" lying around can disrupt your flow just as much as mental clutter can. But sometimes the idea of clearing it all up can be frankly overwhelming, so start small. Set a timer for five minutes and just concentrate on tidying up one small area around yourself; it might be your desk, or your bedside table, or the kitchen counter. Five minutes can be all it takes to get a bit of order in your life, and maybe inspire you to go further.

- Be present. Learn to be aware in the moment. Listen when people talk. Pay attention to yourself, too. Ground yourself with deep breathing exercises and, as best you can, become one with the task at hand.

9. SAVOUR LIFE

According to psychologists Fred Bryant and Joseph Veroff, "Positive events alone are not enough to bring about happiness. People need to be able to attend to and appreciate the positive feelings that emerge from positive events."[xiii]

Example Activities

- Create a scrapbook of the things of you love or find beautiful. Add a short description about the items you've included. What do you find wonderful about the thing? Where did you come across it? How did it make you feel?

- Create a "Wonder wall". Similar to the scrap book idea, but instead of putting pictures into an album, place each one in a nice frame and display it on a dedicated wall at home. This can be a great activity to do with the family, encouraging them to add things to the wall too and talk about the items. Not only will you be able to see these beautiful things every day – but it will also encourage conversations in the family about them, and with other friends who come and visit. This brings an added advantage of having you savour the experience all over again as you tell someone new about it.

- Stop and smell the roses. It sounds gimmicky, but do it, stop and smell the roses. Also, stop and say hello to the pigeons. Walk through the park during your lunch break, or take a new route to work, school, or grocery store.

10. COMMIT TO YOUR GOALS

Setting specific, difficult, and challenging goals leads to high performance. Such goals help us focus. It can also lead to an increase in effort and persistence.[xiv]

But we should also connect with the "why" behind them and make them a personal "why." A why based on what we want, rather than what everyone else wants. A why based on our greater purpose in life. If we do that, we'll be more likely to feel motivated—even when it's tough to go to the gym or spend another hour looking at budgets. Connecting to the "why" allows us to know we are doing it for ourselves not for others.

Example Activities

- Evaluate where you are. Think about your workload and commitments. Think about what you are doing all this for. What is the greater purpose you are serving doing all this? How satisfied are you with them? With yourself? Asking these questions is hard, but it gives you a baseline for forward motion.

- Write down a goal. Now, give it a description. The more specific you are, the more you'll see how the goal intersects with your larger purpose. Does it?

- Remember to be SMART. SMART goals are specific, measurable, attainable, realistic, and time-sensitive.[21] When setting your goals, keep the five qualities in mind. It'll keep you in control, not to mention defeat unrealistic expectations and potential inner critics.

---

21. Just because you want attainable goals doesn't mean you shouldn't dream big. This activity is more about finding the steps needed to turn crazy, wonderful dreams into realities.

11. PRACTICE RELIGION AND SPIRITUALITY

Spirituality is difficult to define in any standard way, which can make it hard to analyse. Even so, higher levels of spirituality—the idea of connecting with something larger than yourself—are strongly correlated to higher life satisfaction.[xv] Spiritual practices can also help you build community and relationships.

Example Activities

- Take time to wonder. Find the extraordinary in the ordinary. Look for beauty in motion—the little boy walking with his dad, the girl helping an elderly woman, the cat sprawled across your keyboard.

- Find a ritual. What activity sets you at ease and gives you a sense of peace? For some people, the activity is yoga or meditation. For others, it's art. Find what speaks to you and make a habit of practicing it regularly.

- Pray. Prayer reminds us to be humble and connects us with a force bigger than ourselves. And it doesn't have to take place in a church. Pray all the time and everywhere, perhaps in an open field where you stop to soak in the beauty.

12. TAKE CARE OF YOUR MIND AND BODY

Meditation and exercise can have powerful and positive effects on the mind and body, reducing stress[xvi] and improving concentration.[xvii] The two activities can also increase self-awareness, which enables self-compassion and self-care.

Example Activities

- Meditate. Meditation doesn't come easy to everyone. Start small. Take a class, buy a how-to book, or use an app.

- Exercise. Find a sport you like or think you'll like. Get serious about this activity by setting a goal like running a 5K or finding a friend to participate in the sport with you.

- Visit with the professionals. Taking care of our bodies and minds means visiting physicians and counsellors on a regular basis. Commit to your health and well-being by scheduling an appointment.

Over the years, I have found that the activities in here that help me most include:

- Journaling (included in "coping strategies"). I journal a lot, particularly when I have moments of doubt or fears coming up.

- Flow. When I am speaking on stage, training groups, or writing, I can disappear for hours. I come alive and the time just flies past. And when I struggle to get into flow, anyone who knows me will tell you that I start to tidy stuff and move furniture.

- Relationships. I can really say that over the last years I have found my people, the ones who really get me and love me for who I am. Furthermore, since I moved back to Northern Ireland at the end of 2018, I have really enjoyed spending a lot more time with my family. It's so great to be home!

And what about you? What activities are you going to give a try to?

PLAY TO YOUR STRENGTHS
EVERY SINGLE DAY

One of the most impactful ways we can thrive is to align to our best selves and play to our strengths and values.

Traditionally, any kind of performance review taking place in a corporate environment will typically focus on areas where we underperform. But studies are starting to show that when we work with a strength-based focus, identifying when things are going well and what the impact is of that, this can work a lot better.[22]

When we align strengths and values, the money and the job often follow as a natural progression. (Or we discover those things aren't *quite* as important as they once were.) However, if we lead with the money and the job, we may well end up living a life that sucks our souls dry.

But staying in alignment isn't easy. For a start, no one really teaches us to identify what it means to be the best version of ourselves, particularly in a value-based or strengths-based way.

Even if we do spend time thinking about what our best selves looks like, it can be hard to keep hold of those images.

---

22. See for example the article in HBR March—April 2019 on "The feedback fallacy," Marcus Buckingham and Ashley Goodall

Everyone wants a piece of us, all the time—at work, home, and at play. We seem to be on the go all the time, so much so that we get wrapped up in what we need to *do* today and miss out on *living*.

I want to help you stay in alignment.

One thing you can do is to use a series of questions throughout the day[23].

- In the morning ask, "How do I want to show up in the world today?"

- Halfway through the day ask, "What is going well today? To what extent am I in alignment with my intention?" (I make sure this question happens by setting an alarm on my phone.)

- At the end of the day, reflect on how the day went and what you are grateful for.

But for those questions to be truly impactful, we need to start playing to our strengths. Once again, a complete overhaul of our lives from one day to the next is impractical, not to mention unhelpful, so let's select one thing to do every day to come into alignment with who and where we want to be.

This exercise will help with that by identifying your strengths to bring you into closer alignment with your best self. In each case, we will (1) find the starting point, or ideal state, (2) determine to what extent you already use them, and then (3) identify the gap and how to fill it.

Don't feel overwhelmed by the immensity of the task. Once again, you have a choice.

---

23. My good friend Ana Lucia Cottone introduced me to these questions.

Option 1

Go through each area, step by step. For the first couple of days, do some journaling (Days 1–3) and then spend some time planning (Day 4)[24]. You'll then spend the rest of the month adding one thing to your day or week to bring yourself into alignment.

Option 2

Read through the different prompts and questions, notice what causes you to pause and think, and then just start there.

DAY 1. DISCOVER YOUR CHARACTER STRENGTHS

Character strengths are inherent. According to the VIA Institute on Character, character strengths are "the positive parts of your personality that impact how you think, feel, and behave, and are the keys to being your best self. [...] They are different than your other strengths, such as your unique skills, talents, interests, and resources, because character strengths reflect the 'real' you—who you are at the very core."

Such strengths generally enrich and energize us. When we build our lives and work around them, a whole lot of things get better. For example, when we are doing things that come easily, we reach a flow state quite easily. We come away from it restored rather than depleted.

Step 1. Identify your character strengths

What are your top three to five character strengths?

There are a couple of ways to find these. One is to go through a list of strengths and see which one resonates.[25]

Alternatively, you can access an online questionnaire with the VIA Institute Character Strengths Test.[xviii]

---

24. Hence the reference to Day #1, #2, et cetera for each series of questions.

25. You can find one on the VIA institute website, for example, here https://www. viacharacter.org/character-strengths.

1. ...

2. ...

3. ...

4. ...

5. ...

Step 2. Determine to what extent you use your strengths on a day-to-day basis

Think about your character strengths. To what extent do you use them on a regular basis in any aspect of your life—business, career, or otherwise?

1. ...

2. ...

3. ...

4. ...

5. ...

Step 3. Identify the gap

Where, when, and around whom do you *not* employ your character strengths?

1. ...

2. ...

3. ...

4. ...

5. ...

What are one or two things you could do to use your strengths more?

1. ...

2. ...

DAY 2. UNLEASH YOUR SUPERPOWERS

Your character and personality relate to who you are. Superpowers, by contrast, are what you are capable of. These skills, talents, and abilities come so easily that you can do them in your sleep.[26]

Step 1. Recognize your superpowers
What are your top three to five superpowers? If you aren't sure, ask others for their input. Email a handful (eight to ten, tops) of close, trusted friends and ask them to tell you, truthfully, what makes you awesome. As you read their answers, notice themes that keep coming up. If more than two or three people tell you something great about yourself, maybe they have a point.

As an alternative or something to reinforce the exercise, you can also start this step by using Gallup's CliftonStrengths assessment.[xix]

1. ...

2. ...

3. ...

4. ...

5. ...

---

26. Okay, maybe not *literally* in your sleep, but you get the drift.

Step 2. Define the extent to which you use your superpowers on a daily basis

When you think about each of your superpowers, where and when do you use them? Do certain people affect whether you display your powers?

1. ...

2. ...

3. ...

4. ...

5. ....

Step 3. Identify where you are and where you want to be

Where are you not playing to your superpowers?

1. ...

2. ...

3. ...

4. ...

5. ....

Where you could use your superpowers more?

1. ...

2. ...

3. ...

4. ...

5. ....

What one or two things could you do to play to these strengths more?

1. ...

2. ...

DAY 3. IDENTIFY YOUR UNFAIR ADVANTAGE

An unfair advantage takes the idea of your superpowers further. It is the one thing you do so well that bystanders watch in amazement. When they try to follow your example, they have to invest a lot of money and a hell of a lot of hours to do what you do as well as you.[27] If you were a product for sale on the marketplace, that would be your unique selling proposition.

You may be using this unfair advantage. But maybe not. Maybe you worry about outshining others or stepping on toes, so you keep your strength hidden. But it's there. It sometimes oozes out, too. And when it does, you know it because you feel happy and content.

Step 1. Proclaim your unfair advantage
What is your unfair advantage? Don't feel guilty or ashamed about it; celebrate it. You were given a particular talent or skill for a reason.

---

27. I first heard this definition from Jonathan Fields of the Good Life Project (www.jonathanfields.com) and found it to be a really tangible and concrete way of explaining things. In my case, and by way of example, my unfair advantage as a speaking strategist is that I know how to take complicated ideas and translate them into a story that human beings can understand. I can do this because I have spent 20 years as a speaker on stages around the world, 16 of which occurred as part of my role as a tax consultant. If you can explain VAT to game developers, you can explain most things to most people.

Step 2. Determine how often you use your unfair advantage on a day-to-day basis
To what extent are you using this unfair advantage in any aspect of your life, business, career, or otherwise?

Step 3. Identify where you could use your unfair advantage even more
Your unfair advantage is a strength—cater to it! Start by figuring out where you aren't leveraging the advantage as often or as well as you could. Write about those situations.

Next, create an action plan. What one or two things could you do to play to your unfair advantage more often?

    1. ...

    2. ...

DAY 4. BRING IT ALL TOGETHER

It's day four. Time to choose what you want to work on.

First, list the one or two actions you identified from each previous day of things you could do more to play to your strengths.

Topic	Actions
Character Strengths	1. ... 2. ...
Super Powers	1. ... 2. ...
Unfair Advantage	1. ... 2. ...

Second, look at all those things sitting there. Admit it, it's a lot, right? It is, I know. I know, and it's okay. The complete list is going to feel a bit overwhelming.

So, let's move through that feeling. Your third step is to simply look at all the elements you identified and choose two or three things that would be the most fun to do.

1. ...

2. ...

3. ...

Fourth, put the two—or three—actions into practice, one week at a time.

- Week 2: Do one of your three chosen actions every day to bring yourself into alignment.

- Week 3: Each day, add a second action to the mix.

- Week 4: You know the rhythm—add your third action to the other two for each day of this week.

This overall exercise was designed to kick-start awareness about what your best self might look like as well as ways to begin building that self on an everyday basis. There is a whole body of research that goes into how to change habits, and one of the more effective ones is to replace old habits with new, positive ones. It is highly improbable that overhauling your entire life from one day to the next would be at all effective. However, introducing small, manageable elements one day at a time would be not only more effective but also sustainable.

CHOOSE TO THRIVE

Arguably, the most destructive narratives we tell ourselves are those that lead to putting ourselves last and not looking after ourselves. When we believe those narratives, we experience illness, burnout, and a whole lot of pain.

But we don't have to continue believing those narratives. We can make a different choice, one that involves looking after ourselves *and* thriving in our careers.

If you aren't quite convinced, remember: No one on their death bed laments the fact that they didn't spend enough time at work. But, they may well lament not spending enough time with friends, family, and loved ones, enough time doing what is important and looking after themselves.

Let's make sure that scene doesn't become ours. Let's choose to do something every day to look after ourselves because we are worth it and deserve it.

What insights did you receive from this chapter about how to thrive and look after yourself more?

What are the next additional actions that you will include in your roadmap?

- To do today?
- To do next week?
- To do next month?

What resources do you need to be able to do this and implement your plans?

REWIRE

I ts October 2016. A week ago, I left corporate life. Over 18 years working in Big 4 companies in Luxembourg and the UK. But now, it's time to do my own thing. I am launching my own business, and it is time to grow wings and fly.

But first, holiday time. With a bit of work thrown in, too.

I am heading to California to the Emerging Women Live conference in San Francisco. I went to the conference in 2015, and it was an eye-opening experience being in the same room as 500 other dynamic and forward-thinking women, listening to a range of inspiring and exciting speakers. I loved it so much that this year I am taking my mum.

And this year, I am speaking. Well, not actually on the main stage, but I am doing a breakout workshop during the conference. I have pitched the idea and won the gig, a short workshop on elevator pitches, "One minute to make an impact." It's about making a short pitch that piques the curiosity of the listener and leads to a more in-depth discussion.

I've run this workshop before in Luxembourg, and during the last two years, I have coached many a colleague in their preparation for client pitches.

Now, I am taking that workshop to California. No stress, right?

I've got this.

Right?

But here's the thing.

I am getting my knickers in a twist.

As I think about this workshop, I start to get scared. I start to bring this workshop into line with everything that setting up a business represents. This workshop is going to be a dry run for my business. If I do well with the workshop, I will do well with my business. If I do badly in the workshop, my business will fail.

And as I start to think about that, that pesky voice comes a-calling:

- "What the hell do you think you are doing? Are you mad?"

- "No one's going to come to this crappy workshop of yours."

- "If they do come, they are going to see right through you; you don't really know what you are talking about."

- "You're not ready. Who do you think you are to imagine your name up there alongside these phenomenal speakers?"

- "Go away and do some more work. Go away and start your business, and then come back and do this."

I am getting so scared that I am getting paralysed. I am having nightmares about this thing. My first days in San Francisco I am obsessed by this workshop, and I am thrashing about in this state of fear unable to move through it. And bit by bit, its coming closer; and bit by bit, I am freaking out even more.

My mum tries to calm me down. But it's not helping.

"You're going to be fine, Jo. It will all work out."

She's trying her best. But it's not helpful. It's only going to be fine if I have a complete personality and career transplant—but it's a bit late for that now.

Have you ever had that feeling of fear about doing something connected to work? That fear that is as real and tangible as being faced with a grizzly bear or hungry lion or, my personal favourite, as real as the fear being up on a 7-metre-high platform being encouraged by my team to jump into a giant inflatable mattress.[28] No one is going to die if we screw up on a workshop, doesn't make the fear any less.

---

28. A team building event a number of years ago, where I thought it would be a great idea to just get up there and show them all what I was made of. Turns out I was made of lots of tears and "don't look at me" statements. Should have cottoned on to this being a bad idea when I heard the two partners refuse to get up there and jump—question of insurance, apparently. But hell, that's another story.

I finally came through this fear-fest about the workshop. It took some loving coaching from a friend of mine and a reminder of the bigger picture: why I wanted to do this workshop in the first place. Remembering the bigger picture helped me to find my way through.

We are so often encouraged to be fearless in business, in corporate life—in everything, really. We are taught to fight the fear and see it as a bad thing. But whenever I did that, things just got more and more difficult. The fear just got more and more strong.

Until I learned to do things differently. Until I learned to rewire out of the fear and into the possibilities that presented themselves to me. And to do that, I had to start to accept the fear as being what made me human and learn to manage it so it didn't manage me.

I want to show you how I did that. Maybe it will help you to do the same.

STEP UP AND INTO THE LIGHT

What stops us from stepping up into our awesomeness and true potential?

Often it is our fears and self-doubts—fears of failure, fears of looking stupid, fears of not being good enough[29].

To step up despite those fears and self-doubts, sometimes the best thing is to pause, identify our fears, embrace them, and find ways to shift our mind-set from fear to hope.

The idea of facing the fear and embracing it may sound scarier than the thing we are afraid of. But it's all about choice. We have to choose what to do with fears. We can let them choke us, or we can step up, believing we are meant for bigger and better things.

Why would you make the second choice? A better question might be "Why wouldn't you?" You know something good lies at the end of the journey, whether it's conquering a fear of heights or accepting new job responsibilities.

And yes, stepping up will probably terrify you at times. But it makes all the difference. The choice ushers us into a life well lived and lets the world hear your voice.

---

29. We all have fears, but they can show up in different situations. For some of us, fear appears about succeeding at work or being a good spouse or perfect parent. When do fears come up for you?

You see, you are unique. You possess distinct strengths and your own secret sauce. If you stay small and hide from possibility, no one will ever know those things. You'll be the proverbial blip on a screen. No one will ever hear your game-changing ideas or perspectives.

That's why you have to step up. As you do, you'll show the world what you are capable of rather than hiding because you fear you either won't cut it or you'll outshine those around you.

It's rock-hard to do that, but here's the thing to remember when your choice to step up gets difficult: You were made for more. And, your doubts and fears are completely normal and human. Once you realize those truths, you can overcome your fears and find ways to manage them.

This isn't a case of "faking it 'til you make it" or "bucking up and getting on with it." Rather, it's a question of rewiring out of fear and into possibility.

You'll have to practice that shift because rewiring is a muscle. I wish it weren't, but it is. Rewiring is no magic wand. Wave the rewire wand, and you'll never experience self-doubt again!

That's not how rewiring works[30]. You'll discover when working on something creative or edging toward the limits of your comfort zone that fear and doubt appear. But if you recognize those emotions as normal, as protection mechanisms with your best interests at heart, you'll find them easier to manage and overcome.

---

30. Anyone who says otherwise is no better than a salesperson advertising a weight-loss supplement for the "low, low price of £19.99!"

LEARN TO STEP UP

Maybe stepping up is a new concept for you, but I'm sure you understand the idea if only under a different guise. You didn't get to where you are today without taking a few risks or moving outside your comfort zone.

Before you go further, think about how you're already stepping up. I'll help you discover that knowledge with an application of Appreciative Inquiry.[31] Once you understand how and why you already step up, you can leverage the knowledge to reach new heights in every area of your life.

1. Define What Stepping Up Looks Like

What does stepping up and into your awesomeness mean to you[32]? What do you want to achieve by taking a step at work, play, wherever? Be specific.

---

31. Organisations use Appreciative Inquiry to identify and build upon strengths to bring about change. Individuals also use the methodology to effect change through a strengths-based approach. The assessment tool comes from creators David Cooperrider and Suresh Srivastva, and as you can see, I use this tool in all the chapters of the book before we start the exercises.

32. We each define what it looks like to step into our awesomeness. That definition can change over time or depending on the circumstances. For example, my most recent step meant stepping into a new role and kicking serious ass. As I sit at my desk writing this book, stepping up means finishing the book and getting it out into the universe even if my self-doubts tell me no one will ever want to read it.

For example, "I want to speak on stage at the upcoming conference so that my peers and bosses see me as the expert in my field that I am," or "I want to form a community outreach effort at my workplace so that I can give back."

2. Discover Your Strengths
What do you already do well? How do you manage your fears and doubts today? When are the times you really need to take your courage in two hands and step up and into the light? What do you do to make that step happen? Again, be specific.

3. Dream about What Could be Possible
Let your imagination run wild. Flash forward in time, picturing what you and the world look like after you step up. What would you be doing in that ideal scenario? What might happen if you took the full leap rather than a quarter of one? What's the wildest outcome that could happen? What does a 10 out of 10 future look like? What about a 20 out of 10?

4. Design Your Roadmap
Use the insights from the previous questions to design a roadmap. Write down the steps and strengths needed to reach your goals.

5. Deliver on Destiny
Now, prioritize those steps, focusing on what is achievable.

After completing the self-reflection exercise, you may realize you're a pro at stepping up. Great! Either move onto a different chapter or try one of the more time-intensive exercises listed here. If you're not feeling comfortable with shifting your mind-set yet or have limited free time, start with the five-minute exercise described on the next page.

PRACTICE: FIVE-MINUTE BABY STEP

Okay, I get it. You're a busy person. You have work to do. You have staff to coach and train, time reports to review, team strategy to develop, invoices to send, meetings to schedule, business development to think through…

And I've asked you to do *one more thing*, in addition to your other responsibilities like feeding a pet or cooking supper. I am asking you to start to manage your fears and move through them.

Hang on. If you're saying, "Oh, my *GAWD*, Jo, I can't; I've enough on my plate," don't worry. I get it. I'm not going to ask you to take a daylong retreat or something.

Rather, I'm going to ask you to STOP[33] and think. It'll take you all of five minutes.

Specifically, think about the one thing that's causing fear, doubt, or anxiety right now. It could be publishing an article, giving a speech, or having a conversation. Whatever it is, pin it to a metaphorical board in your head. Now, STOP and think:

---

33. STOP comes from the Buddify application, one of my top picks for practicing mindfulness and meditation. Check it out at www.buddhify.com

- **Smile.** Smiling relaxes your face.

- **Touch.** Feel your shoes on the floor, your body on the chair.

- **One.** Take one, deep breath. Focus on it.

- **Present.** Practice being present. Maybe you close your eyes, look out a window, or use a meditation exercise. Do what works for you to become present to yourself and the thing that's worrying you.

Once you complete your STOP, ask one question:

If I continue to listen to my doubts and fears and don't do this one thing, what will I miss out on?

Flash forward five years. What would your life look like if you have continued to listen to the self-doubts and never stepped up into the light? What would you miss out on? What would you miss out on doing and on bringing to the world?

Do you really want to miss out?

No, I didn't think so.

That wasn't so hard, was it? If you sailed through that exercise, try one of the other ones found in this chapter. They will help you continue to rewire your mind-set and step into the light more often.

PRACTICE: STEPS BECOME STRIDES

Let's be honest. If we really want to make a change, a five-minute exercise won't cut it. It takes more time than that to learn how to manage self-doubt, fulfil our true potential, and step up.

None of that's a newsflash. But it does mean taking—and making—time to dig into what's causing our fears and self-doubt in the first place. It's necessary, too. A lot of the time, we've grown accustomed to keeping ourselves small and no longer see what is happening or where we are going.

To wake up to what's occurring, we're first going to identify what is going on inside our heads and recognise that other people feel and think the same way. Second, we are going to address those things using different tools.

The following exercises consider three ways fear and self-doubt can manifest.

- "Who do you think you are?" (inner critic)
- "The world is going to end!" (catastrophe thinking)

- "I am the stupidest of all the stupid people." (one-shot thinking)

The exercises also include some tools designed to shift our mind-sets and restore our ability to choose where, when, and how we step up.

"WHO DO YOU THINK YOU ARE?"

The first time I was considered for a promotion from manager to senior manager, the partners rejected me. They said I hadn't worked long enough as a manager to warrant a promotion over my peers.

That's fine, I thought, *I'll try for it again next time.*

And I did. I continued to work my socks off for the next year so that there would be absolutely no doubts about my readiness for a senior role. I worked long hours, demonstrated the strength of my client relationships, and showed the partners that I was prepared for more responsibility. During the next round of evaluations, the partners agreed I was ready for the job and awarded me the promotion.

That's when the problems started. It was like from one day to the next I forgot all the work I had done and how much my clients loved me. I started to feel like the promotion was an act of divine intervention, not one merited by hard work and talent. Sure, I had the previous years as a foundation, but this new role seemed different.

I constantly had this voice in my head being mean to me. The voice of my inner critic.

- "You're not ready Jo, anyone can see that. And if they don't already see that, they soon as hell will"

- "Who do you think you are looking for all that responsibility. Anyone can see that taking charge of client development, your team—that's all beyond you"

- "You think you are good enough to be a role model? Who do you think you are kidding?"

Of course, I was ready—more than ready—and in these kinds of organisations, the bosses don't promote you if you're not ready for the job. But those doubts wormed their way into my head until I started to question everything I did. I feared taking a position on anything technical and always asked my boss for confirmation—despite the fact that six months earlier I had been making the same decisions without any qualms. When I drafted emails, I'd spend hours checking the caveats and formulations, aligning bullet points, and making sure my semi-colons and colons were in the right place. I also stopped proposing new ideas to my boss in case he would think them wrong or juvenile.

I spent my days waiting to be found out. That I was an imposter.

Of course, the words of my inner critic became a self-fulfilling prophecy. The more I was convinced people would find out I was an imposter, the more I made mistakes. The more I made mistakes, the more others started to ask questions about whether I was actually up to the job.

One day, my boss called me out on my behaviour and said, "What the hell are you doing, Jo? You are messing up. Get your shit in order, or there are going to be problems."

The conversation gave me a kick up the ass, so I listened to my boss and began to turn things around, getting my work back on track and standing behind my ideas and my capabilities. But I did that through sheer effort. I worked harder, kept longer hours, and held onto bone-headed stubbornness.

And I have to say that the voice was still there nagging at me and being mean to me. I fought constantly to banish it, but it was always there. And that was hard.

I fought and fought and fought; I worked more and more hours; I put on more and more of a façade about how life was great. Even though my life was falling apart.

You know what happened[34]—burnout number one in 2009; number two in 2014.

WHAT DIDN'T WORK

I have a hypothesis and it is this: that there is a conspiracy of silence around fear. We are taught to hide our fears. If we admit to them, we'll be perceived as weak or ineffectual, so we say nothing. We build a wall of silence, hiding our concerns from the world. Ironically, our silence encourages others to believe that they too are all alone with their worries, doubts, and fears. Their silence, in turn, reinforces ours. Silence begets silence, and our fears multiply.

And so, we are often told that we need to be fear-less if we want to succeed in life, in business, in the corporate world.

And that just isn't helpful.

Perhaps you have heard some of the following advice before. Perhaps you too have come to realise its really not that helpful.

- "You will be fine Jo. You just need to have more confidence in yourself".

  Oh sure, fabulous. If I knew *how* to have more confidence in myself, I *would* have more confidence in myself. And sure yes, it will be fine. But only if I work my ass off for the next 5 days solid, at least twelve hours a day,

---

34. Because you already read the opening chapter of the book ☺

so I am completely prepared that I have read every piece of literature and analysis under the sun.

Of course, that might sound like a good idea—and yes when I am super well prepared, I have a lot more confidence in myself and my knowledge. But on the flip side if I do this: (i) I will be exhausted, won't have slept, and will barely be able to think on D-day itself; (ii) I will have become so completely confused by all the data that I have read that I will no longer be able see the wood for the trees; and (iii) I will train myself that the only way to be confident is to have all this prep behind, but sometimes life throws curve balls and you cannot prepare everything. Take it from me—I've tried.

- "Just suck it up and get on with it Jo".

  God, that is just not helpful either. Of course, there are times when I have just sucked it up and got on with it. But its painful. And it is not sustainable as a long-term strategy. When you are operating in that kind of environment, it's all about the stress response. Every part of your being and body wants to run away and hide, but you force yourself to stay and fight. That's exhausting. Do you have any idea of the damage you are doing to your body and your health by being in this constant state of stress? Do you?

- "Fake it till you make it Jo".

  I've heard that a lot[35], and I have come to realise that this is probably the single most unhelpful thing ever.

---

35. Often from female role models appearing on panels. It seems to be a blanket go-to piece of advice to give. Hell, will you please stop telling folk that. THIS IS NOT SUSTAINABLE ADVICE!

Again, once in a while, why not. Sometimes yes all it does take is 30 seconds of courage.

But long term? HELL NO! I have spent entire periods of my life putting on this façade of "yeah, sure I can do it, I'm just faking it till I make it", and I tell you in those periods, this was not real life. I was putting on a front and living a lie. And one day I lost sight of where I ended, and where the lie began.

YOU DON'T NEED TO FIGHT IT— ITS OKAY TO BE HUMAN

Following the second burnout in 2014, I started to read. And watch TED talks. And work with a therapist.

And in the course of this research and inner journey I read about these fears and how they manifested themselves. I read more about the inner critic, about the imposter syndrome, the devil on my shoulder, the little gremlin—so many different notions for the same idea.

And I started to understand that I wasn't the only person who felt these things.

And for the first time I read about the notion of feeling compassion for myself and for the moments of being afraid[36].

And it blew my mind.

---

36. I came across this for the first time reading the book "Playing Big" by Tara Mohr. Tara wrote this book because she was working with more and more women who were keeping themselves small because of their fears and doubts. I highly recommend this book to anyone and everyone, not just women but also men. She goes into a lot of detail about how to recognise the inner critic, and a bunch of different tools to work with it, as well as other aspects of playing big. But do also check out Liz Gilbert's *Big Magic* and the conversation that she has with fear every time she starts a new creative project. Or Brene Brown's, *Daring Greatly* about getting into the arena, even when the outcome is not guaranteed.

Maybe I didn't need to fight all the time. Maybe I could just seek to understand the fear, and then start to manage it so it didn't manage me.

THE INNER CRITIC REALLY IS THERE TO PROTECT US—WE JUST NEED TO FIND OUT FROM WHAT

In my journey back from burnout, I learned to take a leap of faith, and I am going to invite you to take the same one, too. It is this:

You know that voice you hear, the critical one, the mean one, the one of your inner critic? The voice that is insistent and aggressive and irrational[37]?

It sounds like the only thing that inner critic wants to do is make you feel small and worthless.

But what if it wasn't that.

What if that inner critic actually wanted to protect you from something. Something scary—not so much a physical danger, but an emotional danger. An emotional danger arising from going over the edge of your comfort zone.

What if the inner critic simply wanted you to take a moment, take stock, and work out what is possible or not possible. They want to protect you. Not make you small or break you[38].

---

37. I must hasten to add the voice that kindly points out that in your first year of medical school it is hardly the moment to be embarking on brain surgery. Check out Tara's book and the section that she refers to as "realistic thinking."

38. In their book, *Self-Therapy for Your Inner Critic: Transforming Self Criticism into Self-Confidence*, Jay Earley and Bonnie Weiss suggest that there are a number of different kinds of inner critic, including the perfectionist, the inner controller, the task master, the underminer, the guilt tripper, the destroyer, and the moulder. While on the face of it the voice seems to be trying to make you look small, they argue that the inner critic can help you. Each kind of inner critic has different and combined motivations, such as to protect you from criticism, getting approval, and keeping you safe from danger.

But they just have a funny way of going about it[39].

Instead of explaining that they are afraid (because hell, that would be a sign of weakness) they are simply going to shout and scream at you and convince you not to do it by being mean and belittling you and telling you are not good enough.

Are you willing to take that leap of faith?[40]

If you are, I want to share the following exercise that works on the premise of that benevolent intention. It's to understand the reason behind the fear, recognise the validity of the fear (who are we to judge what someone might fear), but then accept it and move on.

To do that, I ask you to take a step outside yourself, create a picture of your inner critic, and then have a grown up and compassionate conversation with them.[41]

Step 1: Recognise the trigger

I want you to get very specific about the context of this inner critic that shows up.

- What are the situations where this inner critic shows up?

- What exactly do they say?

- Think of a specific example and note down the circumstances and detail.

---

39. Funny peculiar. Not funny ha-ha.

40. Of course, if that was a real "external" person being so mean and vindictive to you, I would hope you would be telling them to take a hike because you don't want that toxic energy around you. But guess what? We're stuck with them. They came with the package deal that is being human, so we just have to deal with them.

41. This exercise is inspired by a couple of the tools I learned from Tara Mohr in her book *"Playing Big."*

Step 2: Distance yourself from the inner critic by drawing a picture of them

I want you to imagine the particular situation you have in mind, and as you listen to this voice, I want you to visualise the inner critic as a person.

As the image starts to get clearer, draw a picture of the inner critic. Think about it as though you are doing a sketch for the police after a particular incident.

Don't think about it too much, just draw what you see.

If you don't like drawing, an alternative is to use pictures from magazines to make an identikit.

One way to do that is to cut out different facial features from magazines, like the eyes, nose, mouth, hair etc and then use these to create the face.

Alternatively use images and pictures that represent the inner critic, even if they are not faces as such. They might be images that represent how the inner critic makes you feel, or about what it says, or about when the inner critic crops up.

Remember, it is perfectly conceivable that you will have different inner critics that pop up in different situations. For example, Brainy Bob is there when I have doubts about my work or career (see below), but when I have my fears about relationships or that I will never find someone to share my life with, Popular Penny comes a-calling. You know the one, the bitchy girl from high school that had a string of boyfriends and would make fun of me for being a geek and having no boyfriend.

BRAINY BOB THE BORING BARRISTER

Over the last number of years, I have come to know my work inner critic very well indeed, as well as the different ways he shows up. My inner critic is Boring Bob the Brainy Barrister. He is middle-aged and sits in his office every night until 3 a.m., surrounded by overflowing in-trays and legal texts. He wears a pin-striped suit, the jacket is off and over the back of his chair,[42] his tie is dishevelled, and the squash bag he carries to work every day on a point of principle hasn't been used for at least a year.

Some people have been surprised when I mention that my inner critic is a man. It's an interesting point, and I think it is due to the fact that I worked in a male dominated area—tax and accounting—for nearly twenty years. Starting work in the 90s, I am at the tail end of a generation of female leaders who were taught that to succeed you had to act like a man. The male characteristics of assertiveness, competition, and negotiation were always much more appreciated than the more feminine leadership qualities of empathy, collaboration, and co-creation. Things are changing in today's world, but those reflexes (and the male inner critic) remain.

As I have become more adept at recognising my inner critic, I have also started to notice he crops up at the strangest times. There are times when he rages in my ear. Other times, the times when I expect him to be the first on the berating bandwagon, he goes radio silent.

For example, when I draft an email to a client that sets out my experience and the value I would bring to a project—details based on concrete and objective facts—Bob yells, "Who do you think you are? Don't put yourself out there like that. People will think you are arrogant and aggressive."

On the other hand, I don't mind raising my hand and asking a question if I don't get something. I figure if I have the question, others are bound to have a similar one. In that instance, I have no problem with looking stupid, even if in front of an audience of a hundred people. Apparently, neither does Bob. He's quiet the entire time.

---

42. He never lost the reflex to leave his jacket lying around so people would think he was still in the office even if he wasn't at his desk. This was the first lesson we learnt when we joined an accountancy firm in the nineties. ☺

Step 3: Look to understand their concerns

Now that you have a clear picture of the inner critic coming up in this particular situation, let's have a conversation with them.

This conversation is going to be a grown up one. No shouting and screaming from anyone, understood?

It's time to be compassionate, not critical.

You know, if your six-year-old niece[43] was scared about something, there would be no point shouting and screaming at her. She will just get more scared. Instead you would take her in your arms, give her a cuddle and ask her what is happening, what she's afraid of. You would then reassure her that all is ok, and its going to be ok.

So, let's have that conversation with your inner critic. You want to find out what is going on, then reassure them that you've got this covered.

I would like you to do this as a journaling exercise. Dialogue journaling is a long-established technique that enables you to explore two sides to a problem or situation[44], and allows you to get the conversation out of your head, to avoid spiralling down into circles.

In order to emphasise the distinction of the inner critic from the rest of your being I would also suggest that when you are writing down the conversation you either use different colours: one for you, and a different one for the inner critic, or that you use your dominant hand when you write your part of the conversation, and your non dominant hand for the other part of the conversation.

The conversation might go something like this:

"Brainy Bob. You seem scared. I know it's not for you; I know you are scared for me. What's going on, Bob? What

---

43. Or nephew or son or daughter.

44. See, for example, *The Progroff Intensive Journal Program for Self-Development,* or Kathleen (Kay) Adams and The Center for Journal Therapy.

are you trying to protect me from? What are you trying to teach me?"

(Write down what he says. Knowing Bob, it's probably to do with me becoming far too "woo woo" in the coaching I do; so far removed from all those years spent studying law and tax. Bob is scared I am losing all credibility.)

Bob, when you look at me, how old do you think I am?

(Write down what he says. Bob thinks I am just out of uni in my first graduate job, and still green behind the ears. Your inner critic might think you are even younger.)

You know Bob, I am not that kid anymore. I am a grown woman, an experienced business-woman, now. I have so much more experience than when I was that youngster.

Bob, you know it's going to be okay. Do you see that I am grown up now? What more can I do to reassure you? what do you need me to do to not be scared any-more?

(Write down what he says. He might give me a last check to do before I publish a particular article, for example. But I am not going to be bullied into spending the next three weeks rewriting it all.)

Okay, Bob, if I go away and do that, will it be okay then?

(Write down what he says. Be wary—don't let him bully you—but at the same time, recognise that there might be something more fundamental and deeper he is concerned about.)

Okay, Bob, I need you to listen up. I've got this. Thank you for being there at my side over these last years. You've been there when I moved from the UK to Luxembourg, when I changed jobs, and when I left corporate life. I know you were scared; hell, I was scared, too. But it all worked out in the end, didn't it? Sure, things have

*been challenging, but remember all those things we have
learned along the way.*

*And it's going to be the same this time, too. I've got
this. I've got us. It's all good."*

So, how did you find that as an exercise? What insights
have you learned by doing this exercise? How have things
shifted when you have sought to understand the motivations
of the inner critic rather than fight against this fear?

How does it feel to allow yourself to be human, to recognise and be aware of the fears as something valid in their
humanity, but to put them to one side with compassion and
move forward?

As you move forward into new adventures, you may well
find that your inner critic comes a-calling a lot more often.
There is no magic wand solution to all this—and often awareness simply opens the flood gates. But if you can approach the
critic with that compassion to start with, and stop fighting,
that will help in the long run to take the pressure of the situation and unfreeze you.

"THE WORLD IS GOING TO END"

I am sitting in Dan's office with tears in my eyes and knots in my stomach. I'm scared.

In a matter of hours, I am due to be interviewed for a local, English-speaking publication. It's my first interview as the Chair of the British Chamber of Commerce for Luxembourg. Not only that, it's my first interview, ever.

Throughout my professional career, the rules were clear: "You don't talk to journalists." You let the press relations department handle the press because they were very good at it.

But I don't have a press relations department or even a person. I am on my own. And, yep, I am getting myself really worked up and scared because this interview concerns the Chamber, not me and my business.

And because it's about the Chamber, it feels like if I screw things up, I put the reputation of the Chamber and my teams at risk.

I used to feel the same thing when speaking at conferences on behalf of my department. If I came across as incompetent, couldn't answer a question, or spoke a whole lot of hot air, then I would let the entire team down. No one in the audience would want to work with us, and my boss would look like an idiot because he had set me on the stage.

As I sit in Dan's office, I have flashbacks to those experiences. They don't fill me with confidence. Rather, I am petrified by the responsibility of the whole thing. If I say something stupid—about the Chamber, Members, or Brexit—I will look like an incompetent fool. Worse, the team and council will look like fools because they elected me as Chair. And if they look like fools, well, the Members will start to think the Chamber is a Mickey Mouse organisation with nothing sensible to say. And if they start to think that, they won't come to the events…

Before I know it, I think doing this single interview will bring down the Chamber. A chamber of commerce that has existed for twenty-five years, thank you very much. Because of *me*, the Chamber will fail and go bankrupt in less than six months.

In the end, Dan kept me calm and helped me with my talking points. I went off and had a super interview. Of course I did. But not before I had played out an entire disaster movie in my head.

And I wonder—have you ever had that experience? You have an upcoming opportunity, but fear takes hold with fear-mongering, doomsday scenarios, and Chicken Little replays.

All that may sound crazy, but the brain does not distinguish between what it sees and what it thinks. Research shows enormous overlaps in brain activity when the person actually experiences something and when they are merely thinking about that experience.[xx]

We start to worry, and then we start to worry about worrying. Eventually, our worrying thoughts snowball into catastrophic thinking. Before we know it, the world is going to end, and we are going to be sleeping in a cardboard box under a bridge.

If our brains sometimes project doomsday endings, what can we do about it? Just as with the inner critic, we have a choice. We can let fear take control of our life, or we can realize we aren't stuck thinking a certain way. We can rewire how we think, which affects what we say and do.

To start rewiring this particular fear, we'll want to slow our brains down. One way to do this is by taking deep breaths to focus yourself or performing some mental arithmetic in your head. For example, solve 100—7 = 93 or 93—7 = 86. When your brain tries to do maths, it can't worry at the same time.

In a similar vein, you can repeat a random set of numbers—7,4,9, 2, for example. Your brain can easily recite ascending or descending numbers; it's a habit picked up at a young age. But putting the numbers out of order forces the brain to slow down and concentrate on something other than the thing that's worrying you.

Once you take your deep breath, have some fun. Play the worst case/best case/most likely case game. This is an exercise that I came across in my readings on positive psychology.

The objective of this exercise is to reach the ridiculous. When you do, you'll be able to see the humour and outlandishness of where our brain can take us. The exercise will also give you some perspective, lead to a more realistic vision of the future, and outline an action plan to make your vision a reality.

Step 1. What is the trigger?
What event or comment triggers your worry response?

In my earlier story, it was an interview with a magazine.

Step 2. What thoughts came up with your worst-case scenarios?
List the thoughts that come up for you.

Thoughts	Percentage
I will say something stupid about the Chamber, the Members, or Brexit,[45] and I will look like an incompetent fool.	
The team and council will look like fools because they elected me to the role.	
The Members will think the Chamber is a Mickey Mouse organisation with nothing sensible to say.	
The Members won't come to any more events.	
The Chamber will go bust.	

Step 3. What is the likelihood that the original event will lead to your imagined worst-case result?

This is where we are going to do a reality check. I want you to quantify the likelihood. Take each of the thoughts you had, put them in the context of the triggering event, and ask, "What is the percentage that this one action will lead to this result?"

A quick caveat: I am not asking for a scientific calculation for this percentage. Go with your feeling on it.

For example, what is the likelihood that doing the interview will lead to saying something stupid or looking like a fool?

Well, doing an interview does not 100% mean that I will say something stupid. (If I am not prepared properly or don't think about the interview sensibly, I might well say something foolish. However, that wasn't the question.)

---

45. Brexit: the exit of the United Kingdom from the European Union.

So, let's say I have a 5% chance of saying something terribly embarrassing. I then come up with percentages for the other scenarios, up to the British Chamber of Commerce for Luxembourg going bust.

It's highly unlikely that doing the interview that will make the Chamber go out of business, so let's give that storyline a big, fat zero.

Thoughts	Percentage
I will say something stupid about the Chamber, the Members, or Brexit, and I will look like an incompetent fool.	5
The team and council will look like fools because they elected me to the role.	5
The Members will think the Chamber is a Mickey Mouse organisation with nothing sensible to say.	2
The Members won't come to any more events.	0
The Chamber will go bust.	0

Thinking about the interview in this way helps me to see that it's not because I do the interview that bad things happen. I would have to be completely unprepared or use no common sense for that to happen.

Step 4. What are the ridiculously best-case scenarios that could happen?
So, we have thought about the worst-case scenario. Now I want you to think about the best case. But not the normal,

run-of-the-mill best case. No, envision the most outlandish, appear-on-the-Oprah-Winfrey-show best-case scenario.

Let's use my interview as an example again.

Thoughts	Percentage
I do the interview, and everyone sees me as super smart, intelligent, and competent.	
More people find out about the Chamber and see it is a super-duper organisation.	
In six months, we have ten times more members and are pulling in people hand over fist.	
We are so successful as a Chamber that I appear on the front of Time magazine as one of the movers and shakers in the British Chamber circle.	
The British Prime Minister sees the article and realises that I alone can help her finalise negotiations on Brexit.	
I become a world-renowned negotiator of political wheeling and dealing and get invited on the Oprah Winfrey show. (Obviously.)	
Jude Law sees me on the Oprah Winfrey show and realises we were meant to be together. He turns up at my house (a penthouse in Manhattan, thank you), proposes, and we live happily ever after.	

Step 5. What is the likelihood that the original event will lead to your imagined best-case result?

Once again, it's time to think about your "triggering" event and assess the likelihood of the imagined outcome. Also again, the outcome must occur in the context of the original event, not the hypothetical chain of events leading up to it.

So, what is the percentage that my doing the interview will cause everyone to see me as super smart and highly competent? Well, if I prepare well, my percentage could be 70%. But that's not the question—preparing well is part of that chain of events, not the triggering event. So, let's say the likelihood is 20%.

As before, I work through all my thoughts. Jude Law showing up at my penthouse? Hmmm, probably minus 50. Okay, okay, no minuses, so let's say zero.

Thoughts	Percentage
I do the interview, and everyone sees me as super smart, intelligent, and competent.	20
More people find out about the Chamber and see it is a super-duper organisation.	15
In six months, we have ten times more members and are pulling in people hand over fist.	0[46]
We are so successful as a Chamber that I appear on the front of Time magazine as one of the movers and shakers in the British Chamber circle.	0

---

46. Maybe a few more members, but ten times more? Unlikely in the extreme.

Thoughts	Percentage
The British Prime Minister sees the article and realises that I alone can help her finalise negotiations on Brexit.	0
I become a world-renowned negotiator of political wheeling and dealing and get invited on the Oprah Winfrey show. (Obviously.)	0
Jude Law sees me on the Oprah Winfrey show and realises we are meant to be together. He turns up at my house (a penthouse in Manhattan, thank you), proposes, and we live happily ever after.	0

Why am I asking you to come up with ridiculously mad best-case scenarios? There are a couple of reasons.

- First, laughter and ridiculousness are great ways to bring you out of a downward spiral of catastrophe thinking.

- Second, our propensity to think negatively can take us to the worst case by reflex. By going to the opposite and ridiculous extreme, you can set aside the worst case and move forward to something more realistic.

- Third, realising your best-case scenarios are preposterous helps you see that your negative thoughts are equally bizarre.

Step 6. What is the most likely scenario?

We have worked through worst and best-case scenarios. How about thinking through what is realistic, along with how likely those realistic outcomes are?

Getting realistic about things is not thinking everything will be fine and dandy. It's stepping back onto solid ground and getting honest about what it will take to turn our dreams and goals into realities. Most of the time, it means we will need to work hard to make things turn out the way we want.

So, if I take this interview, what will most likely happen?

- The interviewer is not there to trip me up. The publication wants to ask about my stepping into the role of Chair at the Chamber, so they likely want to know a bit more about me.

- It is likely the interviewer will ask about Brexit, the recent event a Hollywood actor attended, and my vision for the Chamber.

- If I am well prepared and confident, the interview will reflect my talking points and establish my credibility and authority. It will also have a flavour for what is to come within the Chamber.

- The piece is of general interest to Chamber Members and perhaps people who know me. But at the end of the day, this interview is not going to change the course of modern history. Today's news is tomorrow's fish and chips wrapping.[47]

Step 7. What is the likelihood that the original event will lead to your imagined most-likely result?
Looking through the most likely scenarios, they are at least 90% likely. That high of a percentage means the outcomes are also realistic, achievable, and completely manageable.

---

47. A very British treat: fish and chips wrapped up in newspaper.

To make sure your imagined outcomes are likely, too, run the same exercise. Take each of the thoughts and put them in the context of your triggering event. If they reach the 90% mark, congratulations; you have found the most likely outcomes.

Step 8. Build your action plan for the best possible outcome.

You've identified your most likely scenarios. Great! Now what? Well, those scenarios *could* happen. But a lot rests on that "could," namely you. What actions can you take to ensure an optimum and realistic outcome?

For me, in the interview context, the optimum scenario happens when I come across as competent and prepared and cast a vision for the future. But for those things to occur, I need to do some things:

- Get clear on how I will present myself, my background, and what I bring to the role.

- Have clear talking points in place about Brexit and the Chamber's future activities.

- Practice delivering my talking points.

- Arrive early so I'm relaxed when I meet with the journalist.

- Ask the journalist to send a copy of the article before publication so I can check messages and provide feedback if appropriate.

What about you? What are the worst, ridiculously best, most likely, and optimum scenarios in the situation that is causing you worry and stress? What do you need to do to optimise your chances of success?

This exercise takes practice. Stepping back and walking through to the most likely outcome doesn't usually come naturally. More often, we enter stress mode and then down the rabbit hole of catastrophe thinking we go. But if we can still our breathing, slow down, and focus, we will not only find our optimum scenarios but also the actions needed to bring them to life.

"I AM THE STUPIDEST OF ALL STUPID PEOPLE"

My kitchen is awash with sticky notes: Words of wisdom to get me to kick some ass and keep going when doubt appears and asks, "What on earth have you done? Leaving corporate life to start your own business?!"

The past two years in entrepreneur mode have revealed a lot.

I know what I'm capable of. I can build office furniture,[48] work out my IT without a helpdesk, create new and fun programmes, establish processes, and type on my laptop while a cat sleeps on my wrist.

And I know what I am afraid of.

- I am afraid of being mediocre[49]

- I am afraid of being lazy[50]

- I am afraid of not getting things right

---

48. You know this is a big deal if you've ever bought anything from Ikea.

49. My work is important in the world. What happens if I am no good at it?

50. Coming out of the structure of going to a corporate job every day for eighteen years, I was terrified I would sit on the sofa, watch Netflix while eating a big box of chocolate, and surface a year later having done a big, fat zero in my business.

I have always been an A student, and I have only failed three exams in my life.[51] One happened when I was eight years old. I came in twenty-first in the class on my maths exam. The other two happened when I was older; I failed two exams when I was studying law in France during my Erasmus year.[52]

I am used to being told that I am bright, talented, and good at things. As a result, I have a track record of not doing things if I can't get them right straight away. I do not want to create situations where other people could see me fail or where I am not the brightest and most talented.

For example, I stopped my cello classes after three lessons because I couldn't figure the strings immediately. Italian lessons lasted about three weeks, too. The idea of learning and practicing vocabulary every day felt like too much of an effort. I wanted to be fluent in the language from one day to the next. And, because I refused to fall over when learning to water ski, I zipped around the bay looking like a constipated duck.

For precisely the same reason, I did not write a business plan when I started my own business. Now, this might sound bonkers, but it's a fact. I preferred to start my business on the blind faith that I would work out how to create a viable and successful business. I would rather do that than write a business plan that might be wrong.

But then I went to Austin for an entrepreneurship programme. There, I learned it was okay to get things wrong. I experienced this breakthrough during a session about lean

---

51. Bearing in mind I have spent nearly twenty-five years studying at school, university, and law school, and for tax qualifications in two jurisdictions, that's not bad.

52. The Erasmus programme: a European programme for students to spend a year of their university degree studying in a European city alongside the local students and under local conditions.

canvases.[53] I'd heard of the concept, but I'd yet to work on a canvas—I was too terrified of getting it wrong.

The session facilitator, though, said something so profound that it changed my approach. He said, "Whatever you write on this lean canvas, 95% of it will be completely wrong. And that's okay."

It blew my mind to be told I could be wrong, and it would be okay! Somehow, I'd got it into my head that when you wrote this kind of plan, you only got one go at it. But that's not true at all. The facilitator explained that most entrepreneurs have an entire file of lean canvases because business plans change over time as the ideas get out into the universe to be tested by real-life clients. And, different business stages require new lean canvases. I could expect to write, correct, and amend my canvas over and over again.

Did I believe him? Not exactly. Sure, I believed 95% of my canvas would likely be wrong. But I had more of a challenge believing it was okay to be wrong. Forty-odd years of believing I had to know how to do it and how to get it right weren't going to disappear on his say-so.

But I decided to take a leap of faith. I would believe it was okay to try, and, if I tested the canvas and realised it wasn't right, I could try again. I would also look at the incorrect canvas and see what I could learn from it.

I would treat the whole thing as though I were a scientist. I thought, *What if I view this process as a laboratory for discovery, a bit like a scientist with his experiments? What can I learn from this experience?*

So, I wrote my first lean canvas, and I came back from Austin with a new sticky note for my kitchen:

---

53. A lean canvas is a streamlined business overview that sets out the key elements of your business plan on a single page.

*"Nothing is set in stone. If it doesn't work, I will
simply try a different way."*

What about you? Are there situations where you are offered
an opportunity, but you decide not to take it for fear of getting
it wrong? Are you so used to getting things right and being
good at things that if you receive negative feedback about
something or something goes wrong that it shakes your confidence completely?

If so, then this exercise is for you. It'll give you the courage
to not get everything right and to see the opportunity in the
times when things don't work out as we think they should.

MIND-SET

Before I jump into the exercises, I want to pause and talk
about mind-set briefly.

According to Carol Dweck,[xxi] a mind-set is a "belief about
yourself and your most basic qualities". You construct it every
day, usually without noticing it. It's based on social norms
learned at home and school and reinforced by messages we
receive, particularly in terms of praise.

More specifically, your mind-set will determine whether
you see your qualities and talent as something fixed in stone
or something that can be built upon.

There are two types of mind-set: fixed and growth. Someone
with a fixed mind-set believes some people are smart and some
people aren't. That's just the way the world is. If they fail at
something, they are likely to think, "You see, I am clearly the
stupidest person on planet Stupid." That, or they think, "I
am not good enough."

A growth mindset operates on the basis that things change
and ability is malleable. A person with a growth mindset who
experiences failure thinks, "I failed this time, but I can try again."

Understanding whether we have a fixed or growth mind-set can help us understand why we react to criticism and particular situations in a certain manner.

- A fixed mind-set doesn't want to hear criticism and will often ignore or challenge feedback. Someone with a fixed mind-set may also fear criticism, seeing it as a sign of ultimate failure.

- A growth mind-set sees criticism and feedback as essential to growth and development. It embraces criticism, considering it an opportunity to improve or try again.

WHO CARES ANYWAY?

So, why am I talking about mind-sets, and why should you care? I want to highlight mind-sets because, when we are in a fixed one and don't want to hear criticism, we sometimes freeze in fear of criticism and feedback. We keep our ideas small and to ourselves rather than get our ideas out into the world because we believe we only have one shot at getting them right.

Other times, we start something, like a new business or a qualification that will help us move forward. But when the work gets too difficult, we give up because we're afraid all our work will only end in disastrous failure. In so doing, we limit our ultimate potential.

Or we might work really hard on something—a new idea, an article, a blog—and we are really proud of it. We know we tried our best. We send it out into the world, but nothing happens right away. No one says, "Great job." All of a sudden, the doubts crop up. We wonder if our work is any good and only sigh in relief when we receive external validation. We have lost sight of our North Star and only feel we have succeeded when others deem it so, not when we have learned something that can help us grow even more.

When we experience any of the "I'm stuck" moments described here, an excellent tool is learning to shift—rewire—from a fixed mind-set to a growth mind-set.

CHOOSE A DIFFERENT PATH

As you sit there stressing about publishing a post, presenting a new idea to your boss, or delivering a keynote speech in front of 500 people, know you have done all the double checks you need to do—nothing needs to be changed, evaluated, or amended. The only thing stopping you now is a fear of criticism or getting it wrong.

Easy peasy, right? All you need to do is move past your fear of criticism and move from a fixed to a growth mind-set.

You're probably not thinking that. Your thoughts may be closer to this statement: "Great, Jo. Now how do you want me to do that?"

I recommend using the following thought process, which can be found in Carol Dweck's book.

- Recognise when you think in black and white terms in a fixed mind-set way. When you think like this, you approach every action as something others will like or won't like. "If they don't like it, I am a failure. If they do like it, I am a success. It is all down to them. I have no say in the matter."

- Recognise you have a choice. You could get stuck with the idea you can't do anything to change things, or you could see this time and place as a possibility to grow.

- Ask a different question in a growth mind-set voice. "What do I want to learn about my ideas? What could I learn if I share them with the world? How might I use feedback, negative and positive, to grow and move forward?"

- Take the growth mind-set action: Hit the damn publish button![54]

Once you walk through this thought process and hit the publish button, you'll start to receive feedback. But what should you do with it? I suggest using it to learn and grow and keep moving forward.

Step 1. What information do you get from the feedback?
Let's be factual: List the feedback you received. Think about it.

Try to dig deeper if you need to clarify the feedback. For example, "I liked it" isn't very helpful. You know the person liked *something*, but what and why? Is it that your underlying notion summed up exactly what they were thinking? Or is it because the steps you gave were tangible and practical? Maybe it's something more aesthetic like using blue text instead of black. Or maybe you made them think in a different way?

When it comes to feedback, you want specifics. If you don't have any specifics, ask for them. Find out what a person liked about your speech or article.

Now, take a look at the feedback and think through these questions.

- Who is giving the feedback? Are they people whose feedback is important, such as your stakeholders,[55] potential or existing clients, bosses, or audience members?

---

54. For the purposes of this exercise, let's think about the idea of hitting the publish button as being not just the article, but an analogy to also send the email setting out your idea or getting up on stage to deliver the keynote.

55. Stakeholders: the people whom you impact with your work, and those who impact you. Note: Stakeholders do not necessarily include your parents!

- If receiving feedback from stakeholders,[56] what does their feedback tell you about what's important to them? Are there priorities you can do something about?

- What does the feedback tell you about assumptions you might have made? Does the feedback give you new facts to think about?

- What are your choices now?

Step 2. How can you translate the feedback into concrete action points that help you move forward?
In order for feedback from your stakeholders to be truly helpful—i.e., it helps you move forward—you will need to translate the feedback into something you can work with.

How do you do that? Well, let's work though a couple of examples.

First example, you receive negative feedback on a blog. The person says the steps listed in it were wishy-washy and impossible to work with. To translate that feedback into something useful and practical, you might ask:

- How can I make the steps more tangible?

- What exercises have I done with clients that have been successful?

- What can I use from those exercises to improve the steps in my blog?

- How can I get out of my head or books and into concrete steps?

---

56. If the feedback is from someone other than a stakeholder, it's decision time: Do you want to implement that feedback or set it aside (if only momentarily)?

Another example: You get feedback that your one-day workshop did not cover the things the client wanted to cover, did not have enough breaks, and did not enough room to practice. Oof, that's a lot. Let's break all that feedback down with some questions.

- What could you do to discover your clients' objectives so that future workshops cover the right points?

- Where could you put in more breaks and practice time in the programme?

- Does it make sense to break things into different sessions?

Asking simple questions like those give you much-needed information and specific action steps. All you need to do is follow-through on your answers and action plans to turn negatives into positives.

Step 3. What are your next steps in your learning journey?
Finish your review with a couple of final questions.

- What insights have you received from this feedback?

- How do you feel about that post, speech, or work-shop now?

- How do you move forward?

We've seen three ways fears and doubt show up. Of course, there are others. But the ones shared here present a good sample size. How will you incorporate their ideas in your overall journey?

MOVE FROM FEAR TO POSSIBILITY

Before we leave this chapter on rewiring, I want to say one last thing.

Do not believe that critical, catastrophe thinking or one-shot thinking will vanish now that you recognise and have named your doubts and fears. Lordy, we should be so lucky.

The opposite may actually happen now that you've named your fears. Now they seem to pop up on every street corner and in every alleyway.

But they aren't necessarily the same-old, same-old fears, and they sometimes show up in new places. As an example, my inner critic used to appear when I first published articles on public speaking. But the more I published, the easier the step became. That changed when I wanted to write about my burnout. Brainy Bob the Boring Barrister barrelled out of an alley with even more critical things to say.

That doesn't mean you have a problem. Far from it. It simply means you have a word for what you're experiencing and the tools to do something about it.

That's a good thing because you aren't alone anymore. You know other people struggle with doubt and fear, too. You also possess questions and action steps to help you move forward. Whenever you're not sure where to start when fear creeps up, you can return to the exercises in this chapter or review your answers to these three questions.

1. What insights did you develop as we talked about rewiring your mind-set, especially as it relates to stepping up and doing something new?

2. What actions will you include in your plans to move forward?

   • To do today?

   • To do next week?

   • To do next month?

3. What resources do you need to implement your plans?

COMMUNITY

"It's an amazing feeling to be truly celebrated for who you are and not merely tolerated for what you do," said Julie, one of our mastermind members.

Whoa, what a statement. My fellow members and I looked at each other and nodded in agreement. Julie had hit the nail on the head.

We were coming to the end of a three-month programme of mastermind meetings and were reflecting on what we had got out of the programme. Julie explained that, for her, it was stepping into and fully assuming her "Julie-ness."

As she talked about how our support had helped her, something big hit home: Being celebrated for who we are, not just tolerated for what we do, builds rich community and lets us be who we were always meant to be.

The thought was earth shattering. We're often told it's important to have a network in business, but how often do we hear about the need for community and *its* importance? For a place to be unafraid and welcomed for who we are, irrespective of all the achievements, accolades, and job titles?

You see, for a long time in my career, I saw "building a network" as the ultimate business goal. I counted my LinkedIn connections and tallied the number of business cards brought home from an event and took that as a measure of success. When I had a question or need about business, I knew, quantitatively, the number of people I could tap into.

I have never liked networking events; in fact, I would probably go so far as to say that I hate them. Put me on stage in front of hundreds of people and I come alive. But put me in a networking event where I don't know anyone, and I become the wallflower looking at her watch and asking herself how long a polite length of time is to stay before I can head home. But we're told we have to have a network and attend networking events, so I got over the fear and horror and got on with it.

However, when the going gets tough at work or home, or when things are really great and I want to celebrate, I don't turn to this "network" of 1,300 or so contacts on LinkedIn. I turn to a much smaller group of people.

I turn to my *community*, a group made up of a small number of people who really see me, know and love me despite (and because of) all my imperfections, and who are there for me no matter what.

And, oh, how we need this type of community. When the bad days come and we barely want to get out of bed in the morning because life is tough and we are just so exhausted, we desperately need to have real community. One that let us reach out and say, "*Shit*, this [fill in the blank] is hard, and I am finding it tough." When we confess how we're feeling and what we're dealing with, these people don't walk away. No. They let us know they are there to love and support us.

That same community also allows us to celebrate on the great days. We say, "Whoot, whoot, I am king[57] of the world and seriously rocking this shit!" Our community doesn't begin to brag or compete, nor do they think, *Who do you think you are? Don't be so arrogant and full of it!* No, they celebrate *with* us. Our success is their success, and their success is ours.

So, when Julie spoke, her comment about being celebrated resonated. Not because it meant being lauded up hill and down dale for something we might *do*, but because it meant being celebrated for who we were, are, and might yet *be*.

As we walk through life, we need to build a community where we can be ourselves and others can be themselves, too. This community gives us a sense of belonging we rarely find in the workplace. With it, we don't have to fit into some corporate box; we can be our full, authentic selves. And trust me on this, this kind of community changes everything. We walk with co-champions, with people who believe in owning our strengths and making choices that allow us to succeed at work, home, and everywhere between.

---

57. Or queen.

BUILD YOUR COMMUNITY

Community is about **belonging**, not just fitting in. It's about knowing and believing that who you are is enough. You don't need to become an airbrushed version of yourself just to fit in with the gang or to fit into the corporate culture.

Community also is about **connection**. You show up in your truest and fullest sense and let others see you so that they can love and support you.

Finally, community, at least the sort of community I've described, leads to **fulfilment**. Maslow speaks of this in his hierarchy of human needs. He says we need the most basic of needs, things like food, water, sleep, warmth, and security. But to access the higher levels of personal esteem and self-actualisation and reach our full potential, we need love and belonging.

YOUR NETWORK IS IMPORTANT, BUT COMMUNITY IS VITAL

I would be wrong to say a network is not important. As you build your business, or advance in your career, you need a network of people who can offer a helping hand. But these people can generally be thought of as more of the "one-offs." We turn to them with specific questions, requests, or opportunities. We're probably more of our work selves with them, rather than our fully human selves.

To be fully human—and accepted for that humanity—we need community. A community allows us to belong and gives us the strength to keep moving forward. A network? A network will more than likely ask us to perform and may take more than it gives.

Robert Waldinger, director of the Harvard Study of Adult Development, was asked about the learnings from data collected on 268 men for nearly 80 years. He answered, "The surprising finding is that our relationships and how happy we are in our relationships has a powerful influence on our health." He goes on to say, "Taking care of your body is important, but tending to your relationships is a form of self-care, too. That, I think, is the revelation."[xxii]

Other research scientists agree. Roy Baumeister and Mark Leary, for example, studied the hypothesis that human beings need to belong. They concluded, "At present, it seems fair to conclude that human beings are fundamentally and pervasively motivated by a need to belong."[xxiii]

Brene Brown concludes similarly. In an interview with *Forbes*, she says:

> True belonging is not passive. It's not the belonging that comes with just joining a group. It's not fitting in or pretending or selling out because it's safer. It's a practice that requires us to be vulnerable, get uncomfortable, and learn how to be present with people without sacrificing who we are. If we are going to change what is happening in a meaningful way we're going to need to intentionally be with people who are different from us. We're going to have to sign up and join, and take a seat at the table. We're going to have to learn how to listen, have hard conversations, look for joy, share pain, and be more curious than defensive, all while seeking moments of togetherness.[xxiv]

Without community, we flail and often fail. But *with* community we soar. We succeed. We make the choices that lead to happiness and success.

IDENTIFY WHERE YOU ALREADY
EXPERIENCE COMMUNITY

Before I help you develop your community, let's think about how you already experience community. Throughout your life and career, you have built your community in some form or another. Use the following questions to identify where you are strong and where you can use those strengths to go further.

Step 1. Define what you want to achieve
What do you want to achieve in relation to community? What would it look like if you had a real sense of community? Who would be in that community? How would you know you belong?

Step 2. Discover your existing strengths
What already works? What do you already do well? To what extent do you already have a community around you? How do you feel in this community? Do you find it energizing or draining? How does your community champion you, and how do you champion the people in it?

Step 3. Dream about what could be possible
Let your imagination run wild: What could happen if you developed a strong community?

Step 4. Design your roadmap
Using strengths and insights discovered with the previous questions, what should your goals be? What is actually achievable?

Step 5. Deliver on destiny
What are the next steps to move toward those goals?

Now that you have some first steps, consider adding a few more with the exercises found in the rest of this chapter.

PRACTICE: NURTURE YOUR COMMUNITY IN FIVE MINUTES

Ooh, this is where community gets hard. The realities of our lives crowd in as we try to juggle all its aspects. It's all well and good talking about building a community around us, but where can we possibly find the time to create or nurture one?

Well, hell's teeth. Do you hear yourself? Do you really *not* have time to build community?

More often than not, the real challenge has nothing to do with time. It's this: When the going gets tough, the tough dig in and shut out everyone else. We hole up with a bar of chocolate. And who can blame us. When the weather is cold outside, who wants to brave the elements?

I get that, but you do know that hiding yourself away isn't good or healthy, right? You have got to get out and nurture your relationships. Let yourself be seen.

How can you do that in only five minutes? Here's an idea.

Think about friends you have not been in touch with for ages. Send one of them a text or email to say hello. Or, if you're feeling especially brave today, pick up the phone and make a call.

I know nurturing relationships can seem like a lot of work, particularly when we have a lot on our plates, but it's not like we need to some grand overture. We just need to take five minutes to let someone know we are thinking about them and then arrange for a meet-up over coffee in the next week or so.

PRACTICE: DEVELOP YOUR COMMUNITY FOR THE LONG HAUL

I am excited you have found a bit more time to work on building your community because, let's be honest, developing a community you can count on and who can count on you takes time. You'll have to show up, commit to being yourself, let down some barriers, listen to your community, and support it in good and bad times.

These three exercises will help you do all that. While they may read as pretty eclectic, they hold some key objectives.

- First, we often get so caught up in looking out for and after everyone else that we suffer. Our energy goes toward others, depleting us. So, the first exercise concentrates on putting boundaries in place. These boundaries won't turn you selfish and self-centred. Rather, they will help you support others in life-giving ways.

- Second, if we want people to see us for who we are, we have to set aside the barriers that hide our true selves away.

- And third, community is a two-way street. This means you will need to practice seeing the people in your community so that everyone feels loved and supported.

LOOK AFTER YOURSELF FIRST

"You don't have to let him do that, you know," Diane, the horse trainer, says.

I acknowledge her comment while continuing to stand at the stall, talking to a horse. We are having a good old chat, blethering away.

Or, I am. He is trying to eat the jacket I have tied around my waist, determined to untie it so that he can cover the whole thing in green slobber.

And I am letting him do it because I'm not quite sure what choice I have. He's a big horse.

"Why are you letting him eat your jacket?" Diane asks.

"Well, if I don't, he won't give me cuddles anymore. And I really want cuddles."

Hmmmm.

Boundaries, right? The horse would still nuzzle me if I took the jacket off. I probably know this deep-down inside, but I'm afraid. What if he doesn't want my pats and questions about his day anymore just because I don't let him eat my jacket?

The thing is, I've grown up in a family who has always put others first even if it means sacrificing our own well-being. It's a hard narrative to break.

So, I find boundaries difficult. Even with a horse. If he wants to eat my jacket, okay, let him. I can't possibly disappoint him. And if I can't put boundaries in place with a horse, you can imagine what I am like with people.

But here's the irony: If you want to build a supportive, thriving community, you must you look after yourself before looking out for others. Brene Brown writes, "Daring to set boundaries is about having the courage to love ourselves, even if we risk disappointing others."[xxv]

It's no accident that the flight attendant giving the safety briefing on a plane tells us to put our own oxygen masks on before we start helping others, but for a long time I found the message counter-intuitive. Shouldn't I help others first? Then I found out about hypoxia. The instructions started to seem like statements of the frigging obvious: Put on your mask first if you want to save your life and the lives of others. If you don't, you'll lose consciousness and be of no use to anyone.

On a plane was one thing. But my life? I couldn't really see the parallels until I thought about the safety instructions some more.

On a plane, you want to maximise your chances of survival by getting your oxygen mask on in the event of an emergency. If you are unconscious from hypoxia, you are not much use to anyone. In life, something similar happens. If you want to maximise your chances of not only survival but also success, you don't run yourself into a brick wall with fatigue, stress, burnout, or taking care of everyone but you. You do what you need to do. You get your oxygen in place so that you can succeed and thrive.

But we sometimes fail to do that because our responsibilities consume us. Our boss wants us to train the teams and get our work done; the team wants us to bring in new clients and projects so that salaries can get paid; and our families want food on the table and kids delivered to school on time. Suddenly, we're tied up in narratives we don't know how to escape.

- "Of course, I need to put everyone first. To do anything else would be selfish."

- "I am the one who fixes things. If I don't, who am I?"

- "If I don't do it, no one else will. I don't have a choice."

- "I am the only one able to do this. No one else is as good, capable, competent, or qualified as me."

- "If I do it, it'll only take half an hour. But if I let someone else do it, by the time I explain what to do, and they get it wrong five times, I could have done it and moved onto the next thing."

- "If I do all this for everyone, they will finally love and accept me."

- "Serving others means sacrificing my own well-being. That's just how it is."

The problem is, these narratives can become self-fulfilling prophecies. People begin to expect us to bail them out, or they continue to give us more and more work to do. And if we continue on that track, we risk running empty and burning out.

So, choose a different way forward. Model healthy community by putting yourself first. Here are a couple of ways you start doing that.

EXERCISE 1. CHALLENGE THE NARRATIVES

Narratives are the stories we tell to justify our actions, good or bad. In the case of putting yourself first, you may also hear some of the narratives mentioned just before. Do they resonate? If they don't, what are your narratives? What do you tell yourself when you're working late at night rather than sleeping or when you're taking on someone else's project? For now, just think about the narratives you tell yourself. We'll work up to challenging them in a bit.

Step 1. Notice the narrative

When you think about putting yourself first, what narratives come into your mind? List them.

Next, pick one or two of those narratives and journal about them.

- When does this narrative come up?

- What does it sound like? Critical? Demanding? Some other quality?

- What do you do as a result of it?

Step 2. Challenge the narrative

Narratives, if told over and over again, become beliefs. Beliefs, in turn, lead to actions that reinforce the narrative. As such, the initial narrative becomes a self-fulfilling prophecy.

So, let's challenge the narrative in the cold light of day. Ask:

- Is the narrative true? For example, are you the *only* person who can accomplish this particular task?

- If you were in a court of law, could you prove the narrative true beyond a shadow of doubt? What is your evidence in favour and against it?

- When you go through the day believing your narrative, what happens?

- Flash forward twenty years. What is your life like if you continued believing the narrative all that time? What is life like if you stopped believing it and started believing something else?

Step 3. Give Yourself Permission to Follow a Different Narrative

What would it be like to give yourself permission to have a different narrative? To believe that it is okay to look after yourself first?

Start the process by writing yourself a permission slip[58] to look after yourself first:

"I, (INSERT YOUR NAME), give myself permission to look after myself first by (INSERT ACTIVITY)."

If you still find it difficult to give yourself permission, go back to the chapter on thriving and re-read your love letter. You are worth looking after. Believe it!

EXERCISE 2. START SMALL AND DO SOMETHING EVERY DAY TO BREATHE

Now that you have given yourself permission to look after yourself, what are you going to do? If you aren't sure how to practice self-care, visit the chapter "Thrive." It has plenty of exercises designed to restore your mind, body, and spirit.

EXERCISE 3. DEFINE AND IMPLEMENT BOUNDARIES

Brene Brown defines boundaries through a question: "What is ok, and what is not ok?"[xxvi] Sarri Gilman puts boundaries a little differently. She describes them as an internal compass with only two directions on it: yes and no.[xxvii]

Now, those definitions might sound simple, but sometimes it can be difficult to define boundaries, particularly if we're used to living without them. When that happens, we sometimes forget what is okay and not okay.

---

58. For more about permission slips, check out the five-minute exercise in the chapter called "Thrive."

Step 1. What are Your Un-Breakables?

If boundaries come down to what is okay and not okay, what does that look like in real life? Think of the situations or people where you know you need some boundaries. For example:

- Toxic friends in your entourage who suck the air out of the room with their negativity and competitiveness.

- Conversations with a boss who takes you for granted and demands your presence in the office till 9 p.m. while he checks a piece of work that you gave him to review ten days ago.

- The boyfriend who makes fun of you when you don't want to drink wine even though he knows that wine makes you sneeze.

Now, list out what you want your boundaries to be. On one side of the paper write "What is okay." On the other, write "What is not okay."

Step 2. Separate Boundaries from Emotions

When you say, "No, that's not okay," people will react with a variety of emotions—and yes, they might get pissed off or act disappointed. But that's fine. It's better to set boundaries now than to feel resentful and bitter later. Plus, if you establish ground rules now, you'll avoid making promises you can't possibly keep.

So, step away from the subjective feelings. Concentrate on the objective boundaries. Let *them*, not people's emotions or yours, dictate how you act.

Step 3. Assert Your Boundaries

You don't need to assert your boundaries all the time. Phew! No, boundaries, and having to assert them, usually happen at pivotal moments.

- Upfront. As you start a relationship or enter a position of leadership, you may want to spell out exactly what you expect from the other person or people.

- In the moment. When someone clearly steps over your boundary or asks for something that is not okay, you will need to reaffirm your boundaries.

- Afterward. In some instances, you may have said "yes" when you shouldn't have. You either have to go through with what you promised to give or accept or take a fresh stand for your values and boundaries.

It's going to be tough to assert your boundaries. Saying no can unleash all sorts of emotions in yourself and others, including guilt, fear, and sadness. Be ready for those emotions and be ready to stick to your internal compass. Let it guide you toward behaviours and actions that breathe life into you and your community.

As we finish this first exercise, remember this: To create real community around you, think about what you need and what boundaries you need to implement. Doing so doesn't make you selfish, arrogant, or self-centred.[59] It makes you a human who wants to survive and flourish. And to do that, you've got to give yourself some oxygen first. Only when you're breathing deeply can you hope to help other people breathe, too.

---

59. So, what is the difference between healthy boundaries and being selfish or arrogant? This is an important question, and for me it comes from the intention behind it. For me, healthy boundaries are about putting on your oxygen mask first so you can be there to serve others in a better frame of mind and body. Selfish is when you put the bloody mask on but could not give a flying fig about anyone else.

BE YOU

When I was in law school, I didn't think I had the right to celebrate passing my exams and getting a job at Arthur Andersen because my then-boyfriend had failed his exams and was looking at a summer job at the local chocolate factory. I didn't want to make him feel bad or piss him off and lose him.

He wasn't an isolated incident. There was the Belgian boyfriend. He corrected my French even though he couldn't string more than three words together in English and only in an accent so strong that you could cut it with a knife. I, of course, assured him he spoke wonderfully.

Or how about the one who made me feel every idea that came out of my mouth was the most stupid of stupid ideas on planet Stupid? I adored him for years and years and finally felt I had to flee to Luxembourg to flush him out of my system when I realized I had lost all sense of who I was.

Yep, that was me. For a long time, I jumped through hoops, hid my ideas and dreams, and basically tried to work out what the right answer was before committing to a point of view. I was afraid that if I let the guy see the real me, he would leave. So, I bent and warped myself out of shape to meet his expectations.

Eventually, I learned it was okay to be me. That I am imperfect, and *it is okay*. I first realized that in the context of relationships, but I also started to see its importance when building a community. How could I ask anyone to support and champion me if I didn't let them see imperfect me?

I couldn't. So I learned to be okay with all my flaws and occasional oddities.

- It's okay if I am a mad Brit who likes chocolate cake, watches *Die Hard* films, and speaks French with an accent that is somewhere between Ballymoney, Northern Ireland, and Lake Geneva.

- It's okay if I love my job and am proud of what I have achieved.

- It's okay if I have two cats that sleep on my computer keyboard and leave cat hair everywhere.

- It's okay if I look like I have been dragged through a hedge backward on my days off. It's just as okay if I wear three-inch heels and tower over everyone else on my "on" days.

- It's okay if I tell silly jokes and make an eejit of myself on stage.

- It's okay if I prefer to tramp over the fields or through the woods rather than get tarted up and go to a casino.

- It's okay if I know the words to all the songs and sing along when I am watching a musical.

- It's okay if I don't clean the water droplets off the mirror after I finish cleaning my teeth.

I am okay just the way I am. So are you. As the old adage goes, "You just gotta be yourself. Everyone else is taken."

At the same time as *being* okay with the way we are, we have got to learn to *show* others who we are. Doing this can sometimes be the hardest thing we do in a day. It's also the most essential. If we want to make connections and build a community that loves and celebrates us for who we are, we must show them *who* we are.

How do you get comfortable with showing up and being who you are when it's not something you already do? Great question. I'll give a couple of thoughts on that in the next few pages. If you want a deeper dive into showing the world your brilliant self, I recommend digging into Brene Brown's body of work. She has certainly helped me own my uniqueness and imperfections and share them with my community.

EXERCISE 1. DEFINE SHOWING UP AND BEING SEEN

I could sit here and talk about showing up and being seen till the cows come home. But what do those two things actually look like?

Well, it looks different for all of us because we are all different. So, let me ask you. Who are you? Are you already being you? If you're not, what it would look like to show up as yourself, no mask or filter in place?

Now, I'm not advising blatant oversharing here. Nobody wants to know you had toast and jam for breakfast every day this week or what the girl next door is up to. But people do want to know the real you—what makes you laugh, and what makes you cry, and what makes you rise up in protest.

And yes, doing that is risky. Not everyone will agree with your point of view or understand why you're angry about some news article. They don't have to. You just need a group of people who will support you even when they aren't sure why you feel a certain way.

To help with figuring out who you are—because it's hard if you've gotten used to wearing a mask out in the world—use some journaling exercises. And earlier in this chapter, you worked through your boundaries. Those things should help as you look for your fullest and truest self.

Here we go then for those journaling prompts.

- What would it look like if you were to show up as your honest and fullest self?

- How would you be able to tell that you were doing that completely? How would that be different to what you are doing today?

- In what particular scenarios (situations, people) do you find yourself unable or struggling to be fully you?

- What makes it difficult to show up in those situations or with those people?

- What would you need in order to be able to show up fully in those scenarios?

- How can you give yourself what you need to show up and be seen?

EXERCISE 2. WORK YOUR MESSY MUSCLE

One way we avoid showing up fully is by trying to be perfect. We polish and finesse everything about ourselves, thinking that if we achieve perfection, we will be loved and accepted.[60] I think we both know, though, that perfectionism only leads to a constant struggle to keep up appearances. One slip of the mask, and people will see the real us beneath.[61]

---

60. Brene Brown offers an insightful comparison of perfectionism and excellence in *The Gift of Imperfection*. I suggest adding this book to your reading list. Perfectionism is about believing that if we are perfect in every way, we will reduce the risk of rejection, so we want to do well to please others by doing the thing right. Striving to do well and becoming excellent is about doing well for ourselves because it is the right thing to do.

61. If this has happened to you, think how people reacted. Did they gasp in horror, or did you end up forming a stronger friendship? Some people might

To battle the perfectionism, practice being messy. I refer to the practice as a "messy muscle" because it's something—especially if you have a perfectionist streak—that needs to be worked on and practiced regularly. You can't embrace the messiness once and after that all is fine and great. The muscle is not a magic wand.[62] You'll encounter the perceived need to be perfect again, and you'll need to exercise the messy muscle once more.

As with the first exercise, you'll use some journaling prompts to find next steps for being messy.

- When do you strive for perfection? Does it flare up in some situations more than others?

- Examine one of the situations. Why do you feel like you need to be perfect? Are you believing a false narrative?

- How could you challenge that narrative?[63] When you challenge it, what thoughts and emotions come up?

- What would happen if you allowed yourself to be imperfect in that particular situation?

- What is a low-risk way to practice being imperfect in that situation?

- What happens when you're messy instead of perfect?

- What do you need to be able to feel comfortable being messy?

- What insights does that shift in mindset and action give you?

---

react with shock, but most will become steady friends who love us for who we are, not the masks we wear.

62. Bummer!

63. For more thoughts on challenging the narratives, look at the exercises in "Rewire" and the first exercise in this chapter.

EXERCISE 3. ASK FOR HELP

I know I've mentioned Brene Brown a lot in this chapter, but her thoughts on showing up are too good not to share. In *The Gifts of Imperfection*, she writes about asking for help:

> One of the greatest barriers to connection is the cultural importance we place on "going it alone." Somehow we've come to equate success with not needing anyone. Many of us are willing to extend a helping hand, but we're very reluctant to reach out for help when we need it ourselves. It's as if we've divided the world into "those who offer help," and "those who need help." The truth is that we are both.[xxviii]

As you read that quote, what comes up for you? Does needing to "go it alone" resonate for you? For me, it does. I read those words and think, *Hell, yes!*

I have lived a lot of my life believing I had to go it all alone. I was on my own. My job was to help others, not to be the one in need of help. I thought asking for help would make me look weak and destroy my credibility.

I've found out otherwise in recent years. But it has been a hard lesson to learn. As you know from reading about my burnout, it took two burnouts and the suicide of a colleague to convince myself that it was okay to ask for help.

What I have now learned is that asking for help isn't a sign of weakness; it's a sign of strength. But you do have to be completely vulnerable and humble to ask for help. And when you are, people connect with that. They connect with *you*. Now you're human and approachable instead of some perfect person on a pedestal.

But how do you go about that? Because, let's face it, not everybody asks for help with the purest of motivations. So, let's be clear. Asking for help is not about manipulation. It's not, "Ooh, I want to build connections that lead to community, so I'm going to ask for help." Nor is it a question of "these people around me are open and caring; let me take full advantage of their kindness and bleed them dry". People will see right through that. They can tell when you're insincere or just trying to get something out of or from them.

No, to build connections and community, the thought process goes like this: *I need help with [x, y, or z]. And it's okay for me to ask.* You aren't looking to gain anything from the request of help; you sincerely want aid with some project, situation, or person. And, in asking for help that way, you begin to form natural connections.

Before we go on, let's make something clear: You can ask for help about anything. It doesn't matter if it's something big, and it doesn't matter if it's something small. Who am I to tell you what is big or small, anyway. If you need help learning to delegate work to a colleague, ask for it. And if you need someone to pick up some shopping on the way home because the kids have been sick for four days straight, ask for it! Really. It's okay.

Maybe asking for that kind of help comes hard. You've become really good at hiding your needs from those around you because you're afraid they'll look at you differently. Or, maybe you've spent a lifetime thinking you need to do everything by yourself and defined yourself as the "lone ranger."

If you struggle to ask for help, start with some basic questions.

- What does asking for help look like to you?
- What does asking for help mean?
- What makes asking for help so difficult?
- What narratives come up?

- What barriers would you need to break down to ask for help?

After you work through those questions, walk through a concrete scenario in which you ask for help. Guide your mind with these four questions.

- What is something you could use some help with right now?

- What would the impact be if you were to receive that help?

- Who could give you that help?

- How can you ask that person for help?

Asking for help is heavy going and requires using your messy muscle because you risk everything. You lay bare your full and imperfect self without any guarantee that it will work or that the person can give you the help you need. But we do need to try. We will have to think about it every day until it starts to get easier because asking for help enriches the connections and communities we make.

SEE YOUR COMMUNITY

I once had a bias against Big Hair Girls. You know, the popular girls with blow-dried, perfectly coiffed hair.

Blame it on my life at school. I was the geek with big glasses, a bad perm, and a schoolteacher for a mother. I was doomed from the start; there was no way I'd be a part of the popular crowd.

That was all right with me. I might've been the geek, but I was the top of most of my classes. The girls with the big hair, fake spray tans,[64] and perky attitudes? They got the boys, but they came last in class.

Over time, I developed this subconscious idea that being geeky and looking like crap equated to being studious and smart. Looking great—the big hair—meant spending far too long in the bathroom getting ready. And if you were one of those people who spent too much time in the bathroom getting ready you clearly didn't do any study. And if you didn't spend any time studying, what the hell would you know, and what could you ever teach me?

Flash forward to San Francisco a couple of decades later. I am at the Emerging Women Live conference and am surrounded by 500 women with Big Hair. They were everywhere—in the audience and on the stage. I couldn't turn

---

64. The 1980s' version of fake tan, which was as orange then as it is now.

130

around without running into one of them. It freaked me out completely.

But it also reversed my point of view because, if there was one thing these women were not, it was stupid. My perception was challenged, and in the challenging, I started to see past the Big Hair to the intelligence and smarts enclosed within.

The story might seem a bit silly to you. Or maybe it doesn't. Regardless, what's important is that we recognize we all have biases or cases of, "Wait, why should I waste time talking with you?" It's important to recognize our sometimes-faulty sight. By admitting it, we move closer toward seeing others for who they really are.

It's a critical skill for those of us who desire a community where we are seen for who we are. For that hope to become a reality, we have to see others even as we ourselves are seen. We have to get curious and listen to what people have to say. We'll also have to look beyond any preconceived notions about who people might be based on their gender, appearance, socioeconomic status, birthplace, et cetera. Finally, we'll have to find ways to champion and support people.

The next few exercises address those three things so we can improve our sight and build stronger, long-lasting communities.

EXERCISE 1. BE CURIOUS

When you talk with someone, how well do you listen? Not just with your ears, but with your heart and soul?

Too often, our objective in a conversation is to make sure *we* are understood. But what if we chose a different objective? What if instead we aimed to understand the other person and to get really curious about who they are?

Stephen R. Covey helps here with this his five levels of listening.[xxix]

1. Ignoring. You think of the next thing you are going to say rather than listening to the person. 2. Pretending. You patronize the speaker, deigning to listen to their points. 3. Selective listening. You tune in to just the bits you want to hear. 4. Attentive listening. You give attention to the words being used instead of the person speaking them.	You stay in your own frame of reference and never step into the other person's shoes.
5. Empathic listening. You listen with your ears and heart, hearing not only the words but also the person's energy and mood.	You step into the speaker's sphere.

Covey explains that empathic listening makes all the difference. It is listening with the intent to understand, rather than to ask the next question. It is listening with your entire being.

But all sorts of things can prevent empathic listening, such as the following examples.

- Our judgments. We think we are the only one who is right, and therefore they must be completely wrong.

- Our lack of interest. We think they're boring.

- Our knowledge. We believe we know better than them and want to tell them so.

- Our hunger. We're ready for lunch or at least a pot of tea and some biscuits.

- Our lives. We have more pressing matters to attend to. Plus, just think of the world! It's going to ruin, and we might just have the solution to remedy it.

To move past those obstacles, i.e., *ourselves*, let's build awareness, set our intentions, and exercise some restraint.

Step 1. Build awareness

To move toward deeper listening and connection, notice how you listen to others now. Which level of listening do you usually use?

Keep the question in mind over the next three days. Then, complete the following questions.

- Notice whom you are meeting with.

- Notice how you listen to them. What goes through your head as you listen to them, and at what level are you listening?

- Next, look for correlations. Does your listening level change according to situation or person? For example, do you give more heed to a boss' words than your kids'? Does the time of day affect your listening?

- Mark situations where you would like to listen better.

Step 2. Set your intention

You won't achieve empathic listening without practice and intentionality, so set your intention now. Think about people with whom you would like to make a stronger connection and employ deeper listening the next time you meet.

Afterward, evaluate the conversation.

- How did you practice deeper listening? What helped you stay focused?

- What was the result of the conversation?

- Did you learn more about the person? Why or why not?

- How do you think the other person perceived the conversation?

- What could you do better next time?

Step 3. Use an Indian talking stick

Native Americans use a talking stick to manage conversations that could become disorderly. It works like this.

We start to speak about a subject, let's say Brexit. We could have widely divergent views on the topic, so we use a literal or metaphorical stick. When you have the stick, you get to talk until you feel fully heard and understood. I cannot talk, pass judgment, or interrupt with what I think. I just listen. When you hand the stick to me, it's my turn to speak until I feel heard and understood. We keep doing this until we come to a shared understanding of each other's views, even if our views still disagree. That's okay. The point isn't to change people's perspectives but to give them a safe place to speak until they feel understood.

How might you incorporate that idea into conversations with colleagues and peers? You probably won't walk into a meeting with a "talking stick," but you might use the spirit of the talking stick. When you begin the meeting, you could introduce the talking stick concept and use it to guide the conversation in the room.

Honestly, you can use the talking stick anywhere—with work colleagues, kids, a spouse or partner, or a disgruntled sibling or parent. It'll feel awkward, but it'll prevent a lot of injury and resentment. It'll also form deeper connections and, when applied to your community, a much healthier one. No one's hiding anymore because everyone knows they can speak without fear.

EXERCISE 2. FACE YOUR UNCONSCIOUS BIAS

When we meet someone new, we usually decide whether we like them or whether they are any good at what they do rather quickly.[xxx][65] For example, we meet a stay-at-home mum and might think, "She's clearly likeable because she's a stay-at-home mum, but she must not be competent at any kind of job or else she would be working." Or the alternative, the successful business woman: "Clearly competent, or she would not be where she is today. But, gawd, she must be an absolute bitch!"[66]

We're all familiar with discrimination, the act of deliberately treating a particular group of people in a less positive way because of who they are or what they believe. For many years, legislators and businesses have striven against discrimination. Most of us strive not to discriminate if we can help it.

But what about when we unknowingly discriminate because of an unconscious bias?[xxxi] How do we root it out so that everyone in our community feels welcomed and nurtured?

When unconscious bias happens, we're largely unaware of it. That's the point; it's *unconscious*. It's formed throughout our lives and is built upon our background, cultural environment, personal experience, and other factors. So, to pinpoint it, we have to examine it and make a conscious choice to act differently. It's going to be hard and could hurt, but if we don't deal with our biases, we only rob ourselves of the rich community we could have.

Step 1. Find your biases
Unconscious biases make them difficult to tackle, but the Project Implicit offers a well-respected set of tests on the topic.[xxxii] They look at your biases about gender, race, age, and colour.

---

65. That's evolution for you. Our ancestors needed to find out pretty darn quick whether the new person posed a threat to their life or not.

66. Just think how Hillary Clinton was harangued during the 2016 elections.

I invite you to take the test and find out where biases come up for you.

Step 2. Pay attention

Now that you have identified some unconscious biases, take some time to notice when they come up. For the next week, just observe. What happens when you meet someone new? Do any biases engage?

If you aren't sure, these three scenarios might provide some tell-tale signs.

- Have you seen how our consultant is dressed? He looks like he has just fallen out of bed, and he clearly has a hangover. How can I take him seriously when he turns up like that?

- Gawd, why won't he speak up in the meeting? He clearly lacks confidence. I should tell him to be more assertive. If I don't, he'll never survive in this world.

- Crikey, she looks like she's twenty-two years old, and she's a life coach? She hasn't lived yet. How can she be a life coach?

- Cripes, that guy is pretty in-your-face with his attitude. All those tattoos and the baseball cap and baggy track-suit bottoms. I don't know why he is telling me that he has ideas about how he can streamline some of our back office processes. Sure, he's been working with us for a while, and I am told he is a good worker, but really, do you expect me to take this guy seriously? I just want to cross to the other side of the road and run away.

Those scenes are rather blatant, but if you find yourself tuning out or dismissing someone and aren't sure why, you might want to check your unconscious. It could be harbouring a bias.

Step 3. Get to know them

Challenge your unconscious bias by talking with the person and being curious about them. Use the listening skills mentioned earlier. If this exercise feels a little vague, set a goal of speaking with three[67] new people every week.

Try to find out what makes them tick. What makes their heart sing.

That consultant that looks like he has a hangover. Well, it's more that he didn't sleep a lot last night. He's spent the last couple of days working on a report for you and has some pretty amazing ideas—just give him a chance to walk you through it.

That guy who doesn't speak up in meetings? Well, his native culture requires him to sit quietly and respect his hierarchy. He has ideas, but his culture tells him not to dare to tell them unless he is asked directly.

That young life coach—she has seen more life in those twenty-two years than you would ever wish on your own worst enemy. The challenges she has had to face and overcome means she knows quite a lot about choosing a different way.

And that in your face guy with the attitude and the tatoos? Well, the tatoos are all related to his mum, his ultimate hero, who brought him up as a single mum. He left school when he was 16 because he wanted to work and to earn money to pay his way, and he works hard. And he has been with the company long enough to know where it is losing money on the ground in the processes. It has been years since you were last out on the floor; you are too far removed from the realities there now. Give him a chance; let him speak.

---

67. Or a number that seems reasonable to you.

EXERCISE 3. CHAMPION YOUR PEOPLE

Another way to show up and be seen is to champion the people in your community.

Champions act on behalf of other people's needs. But how do you find out what your people need? You know what *you* need—you spent time figuring that out in "Thrive" and in this chapter. Now, use those skills to help your people define and speak what *they* need so that you can be their champion.

Listen, too. You can't be a good champion if you only key in on select words. You need to hear the whole need to crystallize the best way to champion them.

Here are a couple of things you can do to be a champion for your community's people and their needs.

1. Find connections

When you think about the people in your community, whom do you think they should connect with? These might be people who can help them with what they need, but not necessarily. You want to introduce people who can help or spark off each other.

If you aren't sure of the best contact for a particular person, *talk with that person*. Crazy idea, I know, but you and that person will appreciate it. No one wants to be told what they need, and no one wants to be introduced to a poor connection. So, pepper your person with three queries.

- How can I help you advance right now?

- Who can I introduce you to?

- Who would you like to meet?

2. Become a boast buddy

A while ago, a friend forwarded me the notion of boast buddies. The idea is simple: Who are the people who will champion you and whom you will champion in turn? Find these people in your community. Ask them how you can help support them.

When the opportunity arises, stand up and boast about how fab they are, what they are working on, or how people can help.

3. Offer opportunities for them to speak

Besides championing for people, let them champion for themselves. Teach them to stand behind their ideas and encourage them to share their vision with the world.

To do this, think about ways to get their voices heard. Maybe it's introducing them to one of your groups of friends or work colleagues. Or, if you know of a perfect speaking opportunity, let them know about it and, if needed, coach them through the submission process. Don't do the work for them; one of the goals of community is to empower, not to foster dependency.

GO STRENGTHEN YOUR COMMUNITY

In this chapter, we spoke about building a community of people who know and love you for who you are. These people stick with us through thick and thin and change our lives with their support and encouragement to soar.

Before you leave this chapter, look around. Who do you spend time with? How do they make you feel?

Do you feel loved and supported just the way you are? Or do you feel like you cannot be yourself, that you need to fit some version of "should be?" Can you just chill out with these people, or do you feel like you're in constant competition?

If you don't feel loved and supported, perhaps you need to make a change. Maybe it's time to show the actual you. Remember, none of us are telepathic, but maybe that's not what you need. Perhaps you need to rethink your community so you can thrive at work, home, and beyond.

It's your turn, now. What will you do to build or strengthen a community? Start by answering these final questions.

What insights do you have after reading this chapter?

What additional actions will you include in your roadmap?

- To do today?
- To do next week?
- To do next month?

What resources do you need to implement your plans?

STORY

I once asked a client for feedback on our time together. We had been working on a speech he was giving at a conference on a complex but vital subject. He knew his topic. In fact, he was one of the best and brightest in the team. However, he had filled his slide deck with rude words and risqué language,[68] and I felt that was going to take away from the content.

He said the language was for impact, but I knew he needed to bring the slides back on brand and rehearse his delivery. He, a junior staff member, was going to represent the firm for the first time and give a speech in front of about 150 clients. My job was to help him get the message across, but in a way that was in line with the firm's brand, reputation, and approach.

Great, but he didn't think I knew what I was talking about; his feedback made that point clear.

He appreciated the advice I had given him on what the talk contained and how to explain difficult ideas in easy ways. But, in his view, my approach to the audience was all wrong. He took great pains to explain that clients are only human and told me that I had to stop putting them on a pedestal. Sometimes when he was out working at client premises, he said, they would go out to lunch together and talk about non-work-related things. He said that they didn't mind coarser language over lunch. So, why should the language on the slides bother them?

As he said those words, I realized that he was looking at me like some kind of "branding police." He thought I was only there to give him hell about branding as if I were reading from some kind of textbook but with no connection to the reality of client life. He seemed to believe that I had never actually spoken to a client before, let alone get on stage. Because if I had actually spent time with real, live clients, his thinking seemed to go, I would be a lot more relaxed about his slides.

---

68. A few well-placed "F bombs" in particular.

But I wasn't, and he didn't know why because you know what, I hadn't told him anything about my experience. I didn't tell him about my sixteen years of working directly with clients, building strong relationships with each client, and rising to the level of director at my firm. I didn't just go out with clients for lunch on a regular basis, but I had such good relationships with some of them that they would invite me home to meet the entire family. On top of that, I hadn't shared that, by that point, I had spent more than fifteen years as a conference speaker and trainer on international stages talking about complex technical and leadership subjects. I knew the stakes of getting on stage in front of clients, carrying the reputation of the entire department and firm, and positioning the firm as experts in our field.

In a word, I was more than qualified to know what he risked with his bawdy wording.

But he had no idea because I had assumed he would just know I was qualified even though I hadn't actually told him. Doing a good job or having years of experience should be enough, right? Wrong. There was no way for him to know who I was without my telling him first.

I'd fallen into a trap I've fallen into before. I made assumptions, thinking the quality of my work ought to serve as evidence of my skills and qualifications and that my reputation would precede me. I had also believed that making a thing of telling people about my background and experience would be arrogant.[69] They would think I was putting myself out there and getting in their face.

My client proved my beliefs wrong. Because I hadn't told him my story, he didn't take my advice or me seriously.

You'd think I'd have known the lesson by then. I've fallen for the same story over and over again throughout my life.

---

69. How ironic is that: its arrogant to tell someone about my background and experience, but not arrogant at all to expect my reputation to precede me? D'oh!

It started when I was young. I grew up being told to not put myself out there, to not draw attention to myself, to not tell people how good I was.

I got one hell of a shock when I started work. While I was able to go a certain distance with my career based solely on technical genius and peer-to-peer recommendations, there came a point when my abilities and track record were no longer enough. I had to talk about them with others. More than that, I needed to get comfortable sharing my story.

Was it easy? *Is* it easy? Hell, no. In fact, it still feels uncomfortable to say, "I have achieved this, or I have done that…" It seems big-headed. And there have been times where former colleagues have taken me to one side and said, "You know, Jo, you're getting a bit too full of yourself."

When that happened, I had to make a choice. Either I could just shut up and stop telling my story, or I could continue to tell my story but find a way to do so that wasn't too "in your face."[70]

I found a way to shift in mindset and start to emphasise how my achievements benefit others, specifically the person I am talking with, and then the conversation became less about me and more about the listeners. They heard my story and discovered what was in it for them.

I do still find the whole thing tricky. There will be instances where I find it easier to talk about myself and my strengths, and other instances where Brainy Bob, my inner critic, comes yelling at me not to talk about myself, and I just shut down.

---

70. The statement "too in your face"—let's talk about that. The reality is that sometimes when we are trying out new things, we can take things a bit far, and our colleagues really want to help and guide us. And the reality is also that sometimes the comment from your colleague of "you are a bit too in your face and aggressive" is designed to keep you small and stop you from shining. In the past, I must admit that people often didn't seem too worried about the guy who talked about his successes. In fact, he was admired for his confidence. But strangely, a woman telling the same things was seen as arrogant, ambitious, and unlikeable. Go figure!

And there are times, as with that particular client a number of years ago, where I just forget to say anything at all.

But there are techniques that I have begun to use more and more over the years that I would like to share with you. Perhaps these can help you, too, as you find your own balance to share your story in a way that works for you.

TELL YOUR STORY

"Telling your story" can mean different things to different people. For me, when I talk about telling your story I am talking about allowing yourself to step into the light and shine.

You spend your days doing really great work, coming up with game-changing ideas and helping your clients solve tricky problems. You are awesome at it.

Then why the hell shouldn't people know how great you are at it? You've worked bloody hard to get there!

And yes, of course, there is something in there about self-promotion, but does that have to be a bad thing? We have got to get over this idea that its bad to be good at what we do, and even worse to tell others about it.

For me, it is just about finding a way to do it that feels right and comfortable to you.

The knock-on effect of letting people know how great you are is about positioning. If you tell your story in the right way to the right people, you will optimise your chances of ending up where you want to be. Winning the new client, inspiring others, getting a promotion, being seen as an expert in your field.

You will tell a story that resonates with the person you are talking with and you may tell the story in a different way, depending on the audience. The bones and basics might be the same, but the points you draw out will be different because each person you talk with will be looking for something different.

YOU HAVE TO TELL YOUR STORY

I hate to tell you this, but it is a myth to believe that doing a good job is enough and that you shouldn't have to tell anyone. Similarly, it's a myth to believe that sterling work will speak for itself. And it is a myth to believe we don't have the right to put ourselves forward and allow ourselves to shine and be seen.

The problem, of course, is that many of us grew up being told all these myths, so these myths became the truth.

Listen, wake up and smell the coffee. You might not be telling your story, but others sure as hell are telling theirs.

Many of them have worked hard to get where they are, and they deserve all this success. But you and I both know that there are a bunch of folks out there blowing their own trumpets and peddling a bunch of hot air and getting places who are just not up to it. When push comes to shove, if the two of you were lined up side by side, it would be clear that you have more talent, and experience, and things to say in your little finger than they have in their entire bodies.

But guess what, they are the ones out there talking about themselves and getting ahead, getting the promotion.

You know what? Fair play to them. That is their life.

But maybe it's time you got some of the glory, too. Told some people about what you are doing, too.

You have to tell your story because a client or boss can't possibly know everything you do on a daily basis. Speaking your story makes sure your boss is fully aware of everything you are doing, including things not on their radar because you don't work directly with them on a particular project. Speaking your story with a client makes them conscious of how you can help them do what they need to do.

And don't believe people will go out and tell others about you. More often than not, they won't. If *you* don't do it, no one else will—they're too busy talking about themselves and taking care of the things that matter to them. Plus, even if people are willing to tell your story, they could get some of the facts wrong. You don't want that to happen. You want to control the narrative.

So, while it might seem irrelevant or prideful to talk about yourself, here's the deal: If you want to advance in your career and in your life, make the choice to tell your story. You need to be visible to the right people and tell them the right things. It's the only way to take control of your destiny.

Telling your story is important for other reasons, too. Your story demonstrates you know what you are doing. You can bring your clients value. It also builds the know, like, and trust factors necessary to attracting and keeping clients. Sharing your story can even spawn a "me too" effect, inspiring others to make choices that positively impact their personal and professional lives.

PEOPLE WANT TO HEAR YOUR STORY

If you think people won't be interested in your story, think again. People want to hear your story. Yes, *your* story. The world wants to hear your voice because you are uniquely you. Sharing your story, as difficult as it may be, could inspire someone else to be brave.

I get it; sharing your story is hard. I know because I've been there. Talking about tax was always easy, but building a personal narrative? That was difficult, and in a lot of unexpected ways.

I have told my story in different places over the years, but one of the most impactful instances to date have been doing my TedX speeches. The first one was in December 2018, a speech about taking back the choice. In the speech, I talk about my burnouts, about Peter, and about how his death inspired me to change my life.

Here's the thing—writing the speech was challenging, but primarily because it was in French. I knew I wanted to tell the story on stage, and so I worked out how to get support on the language side, then went ahead and wrote the story.

Great speech. Went down really well.

Where it became scary was about sharing it on LinkedIn. The irony. Of course, by that stage, the speech was online, and anyone could see it. But I just hadn't told anyone. I hesitated about doing so, and so I spoke to someone I trust and admire a lot about whether to do it. Here's the thing. She said, "don't do it. People don't want to know you have struggled. They want to know you are a rock star and never struggled with anything. They are going to listen to this and think you are weak."

Her advice threw me off tilter completely and shook my confidence to the core. But after a long, hard think, I posted the speech on LinkedIn anyway.

And then I started to read the feedback and reactions, both online and in personal messages. And the overwhelming reaction was, "Thank you for sharing your story, Jo. Your doing so has allowed me to assume mine."

If ever I had any doubt about sharing my story, it disappeared then.

As you think about your own situation, think of telling your story as allowing yourself to shine and be seen. If that doesn't work,[71] think of it as a means to an end, a box you need to comfortable ticking so you can advance. And, see it as leading by example. No matter how excruciating you find telling your story to be, telling it makes you into a role model who empowers others to assume their stories, too.

---

71. It can be difficult to let go of the idea that to allow ourselves to shine is somehow prideful.

LEARN TO TELL YOUR STORY

To date, you've been able to rely on your technical genius, but that's not enough anymore. To advance further in your career, you have got to tell other people just how good you are and make yourself a bit more visible. It's time to tell your story and show off your skills and achievements to a larger audience.

But first things first. You probably tell your story to some extent already. Let's think about how you do already do that to leverage your strengths and reach new heights.

1. Define what you want to achieve

In the context of telling your story, what goal do you want to achieve? Be specific.

As an example, you might want to make a presentation to your bosses to get promoted to partner. They will want a story that demonstrates why you are uniquely qualified for the role and why you will fit into the partnership. Or maybe you want to pitch your idea to a potential business partner so that they invest in your business. You will tell your story so that they feel confident that their investment is in good hands given your previous entrepreneurial experience and success.

2. Discover your existing strengths

What do you already do well? What already works? In what circumstances do you already tell your story well? How, and how do you know? What feedback have you received when you told your story in the past? What elements resonated with your listeners?

3. Dream about what could be possible
Let your imagination run wild. What could you achieve if you become a better storyteller? What is the wildest of wild outcome possible if you were to succeed with telling your story?

4. Design your roadmap
Building on the strengths, insights, and goals established with the previous questions, what is achievable? In one month? Three months? A year?

5. Deliver on destiny
What steps do you need to take to move toward your dream?

Now that you have discovered some first steps, I would also like to offer some additional exercises to think about and work through.

PRACTICE: TELL YOUR STORY IN FIVE MINUTES

Okay, I know you have a lot going on at the moment, so what's the one thing you could do that wouldn't take long but would have a big impact when telling your story to a client?

If I could give you one bit of advice on that front, one single thing that you could do to help, it would be in the form of a very straightforward question: So what?

Before you recite your entire CV to a client, boss, or team, stop. Ask, "So what?"

So what if you have two law degrees and tax qualifications in two jurisdictions? What does that bring your client?[72] So what if the firm has offices all over the world? How does that translate into value for your client? So what if you have fifteen years working in the fund finance industry?[73] What difference does that make to your client?

Take five minutes to answer the "so what." Write down your thoughts and practice saying them. The next time you meet a client, boss, or team, spell out the "so what" so that they'll want to work with you.

---

72. Here I talk about your "client," but the ideas apply to whomever you are speaking with: your boss, team, or audience.

73. Or technology or manufacturing or agriculture... You get the picture, I am sure.

Now, I must make a caveat. It seems straightforward, this question of "so what," but I realise it is not always that easy to detect. What we think is relevant from our perspective as the speaker may very well be different from what the listener considers to be important.

So, in order to really nail the "so what," you need to figure out what is important to the person or people you will be talking with. Read on, McDuff—I'm about to give some guidance on how to think about your listeners and their interests.

PRACTICE: TELL A (LONGER) STORY

Have you ever heard a speaker tell their story and been so wrapped up in the emotion of it that you felt breathless, inspired, or champing at the bit to work with them? Have you listened to a colleague succinctly explain why they are amazing at their job without coming across as arrogant and aggressive?

Neither one of them developed that ability overnight. It took time, practice, and preparation. Before you heave a sigh, think of the positive side of things: You can tell your story well, too.

If you've made it this far in the chapter, you want to. You either have found or will make a bit more time and space in your busy day to finesse your story. And I am delighted to hear that. I want you to tell your story and tell it well.

I'll help you do that with three things to think about, with a couple of exercises for each thing.

- First, you will think about how to introduce yourself to a client or audience (by thinking about how your experience and achievements will bring them value)

- Second, we will look at inspiring an audience with your hero's journey

- Third, we will look at how you can explain what it is you do in a simple way by positioning yourself as a mentor for your client living their own hero's journey

INTRODUCE YOURSELF TO A CLIENT AND DEMONSTRATE THE VALUE YOU WILL BRING

Okay, let's be honest; how many of you have ever been in a client meeting and introduced yourself by simply saying, "And I am a [insert job title]." No more explanation than that, just a job title. It seems a logical thing to do, a nice succinct way of making an introduction.

The problem is, of course, that a job title in itself rarely means anything tangible.[74] It doesn't actually tell anyone anything about what you are doing in that role, whether you are any good at it, and what that can bring the client to help them move forward.

This exercise is going to be about taking that first five-minute thought from earlier in this chapter on the "so what" much, much further.

We will identify exactly who needs to hear your story, what is important to these people I term "stakeholders," and then think about how your experience brings them value.

---

74. For example, maybe in one organisation a "manager" is one grade off the big boss, and is a role held typically by someone with twenty years of experience in the job and a deep involvement in strategy and leadership for the organisation. In another organisation, a "manager" is someone with about five years of experience who is running some small teams but has a long way to go before entering the top leadership functions.

When we tap into what is important for our stakeholders, we begin to identify the parts of our story that will resonate with them. Once we know those parts, we can draw them out so that our listeners stop and really listen.

Step 1. Identify the situation

When, where, and why do you need to tell your story? Some examples could include the following ones.

- You are on stage talking about your experiences to demonstrate your expertise and position yourself as an expert in your field.

- You are speaking to your boss during your performance review to negotiate a bonus or promotion, so you tell a story to show your achievements and progress over the year.

- You are presenting to senior partners in hopes of being promoted to a leadership position.

- You are asking a group of investors to fund your start-up.

- You are pitching to a client to win the work.[75]

For the purposes of this exercise, identify a specific situation so you can reflect and develop an action plan for your specific case.

I will take as an example the situation where I am going to deliver a workshop on "Train the Trainer"[76] and will need to introduce myself at the start of the training.

---

75. You might also tell your story in writing, too—on your website, in marketing materials, or in a periodic newsletter.

76. The Train the Trainer course is a workshop that trains people to train people.

Step 2. Get to know the specific person or persons you will be speaking with

Once you define the when, where, and why, think about "whom," i.e., the person on the receiving end of your story. In many cases you will know the person you will be meeting with, for example, your boss or your team. In other cases, you won't.

Then again, you might know the person's identity but have never met them before, as in the case of a jury that judges pitching competition or partners on your review board. And there will be situations where you don't know the person's identity at all, such as an audience at a conference. Even so, you can identify likely characteristics about the audience, using those details to build a persona or avatar.

As you think about known and unknown audiences, think about the following twelve identifiers. The twelve items are designed to get you thinking about how the audience thinks, what reference points they have, what is important to them, and what they will expect from you and your story.

- Their role and experience
- Their knowledge of you
- Their background, education, age, and generation
- Their gender
- Their culture and language
- Their communication style—do they speak in generalities, get straight to the point, or focus on the details?
- Their orientation—people or task focused?
- Their expectations and preconceptions regarding you
- Their previous experiences, which could impact how they hear you and what you have to say

- Their lives—what could be going on that might affect their ability to listen?

- Their agenda—I don't mean the bullet point list of things they want to talk about, I mean their personal agenda, such as career aspirations or life goals

- Their questions—what do they need and want to hear right now? What is their pain point (the problem they need solving)?

In my example, the audience will be people who deliver training courses for their colleagues and clients. Some will already have given training programmes, but others will be very new to this and may never have stood up in front of a class in their lives. They are likely to come from very different backgrounds, including tax, accounting, audit, IT, communications, and HR.

Step 3. Identify what is important to the audience

As you go through the items listed above, I want you to really think about what your audience values in life and their day to day. For example, do they care about bringing in new clients, reducing costs, or building their reputation?[77] What things receive their most urgent priority? Just as importantly, what things do they need to know from you so that your story resonates with them?

To help you answer those questions, consider these possibilities.

- Your conference audience who will listen to you talk about a new way of streamlining operations wants to know how you can save them money or make their lives easier.

---

77. … getting a bonus, having a work life balance, retaining staff, learning new things, being compliant with their legal obligations …

- Your boss in the evaluation meeting wants to know how you have used the comments from last year's review to grow and develop and to demonstrate that progression.

- The panel of partners determining whether you should be made a fellow partner should already know about your technical expertise and the business case for your promotion. Now they're interested in knowing how you will work alongside them and fit into the partnership.

- The group of investors you are pitching to wants to know about your company and product. They also want a demonstration of your experience and business acumen—they want to know they can trust you to look after their investment.

- The client wants to know you have done this kind of work before. They also want reassurances that you understand their concerns and challenges and will guide them through the process of adopting a new process or product.

In my example of the Train the Trainer course, my audience comes to learn tips and tricks about delivering training courses. They want to do a great job for the people they train, but they are often constrained by the realities of their day job and the timing implications that it brings.

Having now identified what is important to your audience, the next steps are about building a bridge between your story and experience and the audience and what is important to them.

Step 4. List your key experiences, achievements, and successes in your career and life

Take a blank piece of paper and list the key achievements you have accomplished in your career and life to date. Examples might include:

- Degrees and qualifications

- Key clients and projects, and lessons learned

- Roles and responsibilities

- Publications

- Roles, and key achievements in the role, with not-for-profit organisations

Step 5. Select the most relevant details to answer the audience's "so what."

Next, review your list, asking the question, "What do these things offer my stakeholders?" Keep in mind the points that are important to the stakeholders, as based on your answers to the first exercise.

Once you write down how each experience or achievement adds value to your stakeholders, reflect on those things. Look at your notes and identify three to five points you believe will have the most impact on your target audience.

In my case, my achievements include two law degrees, law school,[78] and tax qualifications in two jurisdictions. The successes may have had some relevance to clients in my days as a tax professional,[79] but they are less relevant today in my role as a public speaking and leadership coach. Yes, they tell a client I am capable of studying a lot and getting qualifications, but probably not a lot more than that.

---

78. In the UK, law school is different from getting a law degree. I have a bachelor's degree in English and French Law and a master's in European Business Law. When I finished those degrees, I went to law school to learn how to put theory into practice. Then, I turned to tax qualifications in both the UK and Luxembourg. Yes, I have a lot of letters after my name. But so what? What do they mean to the client?

79. At the end of the day, it's difficult to advise a client on tax if you don't know the rules.

The more compelling fact is that I have been getting on stage since I was four years old. I've also now spent nearly twenty years speaking about tax, industry, and leadership subjects all around Europe and beyond. Many of those years as a conference speaker were in the context of my previous life as a tax consultant.

That part of my story impacts current and future clients because:

- I have been in their shoes. I know the stakes of standing on the stage, talking about their work, and bearing the responsibility of the entire team on their shoulders.

- I know what it is like to believe that screwing up as a speaker would not only make me come across as an idiot but also reflect badly on the team and our boss. Any mistakes could put the company's reputation on the line.

- It shows I know how to translate a mass of technical data and ideas about tax into a story that anyone can care about it. I know this is true because I know I can engage an audience of game developers with a conversation about taxes (because I have done it on many occasions).

- It demonstrates I know what it takes to prepare for technical speeches while working a full-time job and balancing all the other constraints of life.

Now that you have identified your most valuable achievements for a specific audience, time, and place, it is time to flesh out their details. My advice would be to write out something long hand, just so you take time to articulate the idea.

Here is one way to do this:

"Hello, my name is [insert] and [insert relevant experience]. What this means is that [insert concrete example of how that experience brings them value]."

For example:

"My name is Joanna, and I have been a conference speaker on stages all around Europe and beyond for the last twenty years, including two TedX stages in the last nine months. For the last five years, I have been working as a public speaking coach working with entrepreneurs, business executives, and conference speakers, but before then, my conference and training engagements took place in the context of my day job as a tax consultant in Big 4 companies in Luxembourg and the UK.

Why should you care about all this? Well, first because I have prepared and delivered hundreds of speeches and trainings on both technical and non-technical subjects, and I have a raft of practical experiences and learnings that I am excited to share with you. And second, because I also know what it is like to be in your shoes preparing for speeches and trainings while also doing your day job. I know what the challenges are, and I think I have found some ways to overcome them that I would love to share."

When you have got your ideas clear, practice. Practice in front of the mirror, the cat, to the postman. But get used to saying the words so that they feel right. And if they don't feel right, find what does feel right. The main thing is to one, pick the most relevant experience to the audience, and two, spell out the link between that experience and where it can bring value to the audience.

INSPIRE YOUR AUDIENCE WITH YOUR OWN HERO'S JOURNEY

In the first exercise, we talked about a simple introduction to your client or audience that builds on the "so what" of your history and experience. That exercise was about seeing your experience through the eyes of your client or audience.

There may be instances, however, where you want to take the story further and develop the personal side of things.

This exercise will work on that and look to package your story in a compelling way. It is for times when your personal story is particularly relevant because, for example, it links to the work you are doing or because in will inspire your audience to think or act in a certain way.

For example:

- If you would like to be promoted to partner, during your presentation, share who you are and what you like to do outside of work. The panel of partners deciding on whether or not to promote you already know about your technical prowess and the business case for your promotion. (If they didn't, you wouldn't be up for the promotion in the first place.) But now they want to know what kind of person you are on a more personal level, hoping to gain insight into what it would be like to work with you on a daily basis.

- If you have been running a project involving a number of different departments and teams, talk about *your* personal involvement in the project. If you only talk about how "we" did it, no one will ever know you are capable of more. Plus, believe you me, few of your colleagues will have the same scruples about explaining how *they* ran things themselves.

- If you want to empower women to handle their finances well, talk about how you became more money savvy. Maybe you became so frustrated by the lack of simple, comprehensive investment trainings for female investors or by a bunch of men trying to "mansplain" things that you researched the subject and built an app for women to use.

- If you want to help people avoid burnouts, share your experience with burnout and how you got through to the other side. It will inspire and show them that even if things are tough right now, they will get better.

This exercise will help you build that kind of signature story. Such stories can become especially important when:

- Talking about your work on stage
- Meeting someone new at a networking event
- Writing about your services on your website or in blogs
- Working with a client 1-on-1
- Crafting your bio

Step 1. Choose the right story
What story should you tell? Well, that largely depends on why you want to tell it, the stakeholders, and the situation. But you can lay some ground rules. When choosing what story to tell, think about these things.

- How the story illustrates and relates to the key message you want to get across[80]

- How it resonates with the audience[81]

- How it demonstrates your core values, beliefs, and credibility[82]

In most circumstances, the most impactful stories are the ones you have lived yourself. They show how you have come through a tough situation and reached the other side, along with what you learned along the way. Other times, you might tell a story about how you guided someone else through a rough patch[83].

Step 2. Build a compelling story

As human beings, we have told stories since time immemorial.[84] xxxiii We are literally hotwired for them.[85] xxxiv But how

---

80. Each story that you tell should have a point to it. Stories are, of course, very helpful, but in the situations we are talking about here, there is no point in telling a story just for the sake of it

81. How does the story speak to the audience? For example, is it because it mirrors something they are living or going through at the moment?

82. Stories about you dancing on the bar during your student days, while amusing, will rarely do much to reinforce your credibility.

83. These will mainly be the cases where you position yourself as mentor rather than hero. You will see more of that in the last exercise in this chapter

84. Polly Wiessner, an anthropologist from the University of Utah, has studied the social networks of some primitive tribes, the Ju/'hoan Bushmen. Her research shows that tribesmen spoke to each other about practical aspects like food and shelter during the day. Once the sun went down, they sat around the campfires and told stories. She suggests this discovery shows fire may have not only changed our diets but also our lives. Our ancestors most likely invented stories to pass the time by the fire. In doing so, the fire extended the day and brought people together.

85. Neuroscience research from the University of Princeton also demonstrates how story, told and received, affects the brain. As a volunteer lay in an MRI machine and told a story, researchers documented the ways her brain lit up as she re-lived the event. Later, several volunteers entered the MRI machine and listened to the story. Researchers discovered something interesting: The same areas of the brain flared with activity whether telling or listening to the story.

do we build those kinds of stories, stories that have impact and linger in the mind long after we tell them? To answer that question, we can turn to some of the greatest stories ever written because they can tell us a lot about crafting a masterful story.

Many great stories employ the traditional arc of the "hero's journey". It works extremely well, so much so that many of our favourite stories today still use it.[86]

But what is the hero's journey? Several people have written about the subject, including Joseph Campbell[xxxv], Chris Vogler[xxxvi], and Nancy Duarte[xxxvii].

Their writings reveal a number of components found in almost all hero stories. I have broadly grouped the elements to illustrate how hero stories, which tend to be hugely compelling, hit a number of milestones before reaching their conclusions.

- At the start of the story, the hero is living an ordinary life. He doesn't realise life could be different.[87]

- The hero receives a call to action but is reluctant to follow until something happens, leaving him without a choice in the matter.[88]

- A mentor arrives to help the hero move forward with his journey. As the hero enters an extraordinary world, he

---

86. Take, for example, the slew of Marvel or DC movies. They use the hero's journey, as does *The Hobbit* and *The Lord of the Rings*.

87. For example, in J.K. Rowling's *Harry Potter and The Philosopher's Stone*, Harry Potter lives under the stairs at the start of the book and has no idea he is a wizard.

88. When Harry first gets his acceptance letter to Hogwarts, he is thrilled. But his uncle has no intention of letting him go to wizard school, so he takes the entire family to a deserted Scottish Island to keep them safe from these strange people. Hagrid comes to the island with sausages and birthday cake and convinces Harry's uncle to let him go (even if it did take the addition of a pig's tale into the mix).

meets other characters and overcomes small challenges. Both increase the hero's strength and wisdom.[89]

- Before long, the hero's newfound strength and wisdom are put to the test with an ordeal to end all ordeals. He usually overcomes it thanks to a key piece of information shared by his mentor.[90]

- The hero returns to the ordinary world time equipped with tools that will help him change things for the better. The hero may also realise he always had those tools; he just didn't know it at the time.[91]

BRING THE HERO'S JOURNEY INTO A BUSINESS CONTEXT

Okay, so you are not J. K. Rowling. I get it. But you can use storytelling techniques like the hero's journey in your context.

As you start to use it, you will find you generally have two options when it comes to positioning. One, you can position yourself as the hero. You might do this when you want to show your audience you have lived what they are living today and have come through to the other side.

Two, you can position yourself as the mentor, the person who has the tools, knowledge, and experience to get the hero to the other side of a sticky career, business, or life situation. Here, you recognise that the person listening to your story is

89. Harry goes to Hogwarts where he meets friends (Ron and Hermione), nemeses (Snape and Malfoy), and mentor (Dumbledore).

90. While trying to protect the Philosophers Stone, Harry first encounters Voldemort. He manages to survive the meeting but is wounded. When he wakes up in a hospital bed, Dumbledore explains he will always be protected by his mother's love.

91. Harry might return to living under the stairs, but he knows he will go back to Hogwarts next term. And, while he's not supposed to use magic outside school, he knows it will help him survive until then.

the hero of their own story. You are simply there to help them slay their own dragon.

In this exercise, you will position yourself as the hero of your journey, learning things along the way that you want to transmit. In the third exercise of the chapter, you will take on more of the mentor role.

When you're the hero of the story, you have to show, not tell, what you have been through. By creating a picture of how you have lived what your audience has lived or is living, you can inspire them to act and follow you.

There are a couple of ways that you can build such a story, and each will start with getting clarity on the elements to begin with.

Step 1. Build a chronological story of your journey

The first step to build up your hero's journey is to take a chronological approach and go step by step through what happened.

I strongly recommend starting here as it will help you to get your ideas clear about the elements of your story. When you have the elements clear, you can pick and choose those you want to include or those you will leave out.

The following prompts are on the basis of building a story with a key event—an inciting incident—that convinced you something had to change. And if you made that change, that choice, you knew your life would never be the same again.

Now, it might seem a weird thing to think about—that life changing event—and you might think that there was no single event but more a range of circumstances that came together. This may be true, but hopefully the prompts will allow you to get some clarity on the question.

Life "before"

- With 20:20 vision, when you look back at life before all this happened, what was it really like?

171

- What did it seem like?

- To what extent had the universe already started to send you warning shots (or calls to action) to change? What were they? Why didn't you listen at the time?

Rock bottom

- What would you say was the rock bottom moment? The most difficult moments?

The call to action

- What happened to convince you it was time for a change? Why do you think that wake-up call happened and worked at that moment in time but hadn't worked in the past?

- What do you think would have happened if you didn't change things? How do you know?

- What did you have to do to change your approach to things?

- Did someone say or do something that showed you how to move forward? Who was it? What did they say or do?

Momentum

- What things did you put in place to start changing things?

- How easy was it to do this? What did you do to set yourself up to succeed?

- What trainings and resources did you invest in to get through the struggle?

- Where did you find help and support to get through?

Action

- What did you do to solve the challenges you were facing?

- What did you learn from the experience? About the world, about yourself, about others?

- Were there elements that you learned about that you already knew but just didn't understand the full implications of?

- How have you translated your action steps into a plan that helps people get through similar circumstances?

Success and insights

- How is your life different and better now?

- What other insights have you gained from this whole journey?

- Who else benefits from the change in your life?

- How can people follow in your footsteps?

Step 2. Write the script for the story

Now that you have worked through the different steps and prompts, it is time to build a script for the story. What we want to avoid is a story that comprises a number of "and then this happened ... and then ... and then...."

Here are a couple of suggestions of how you might want to do this:

(a) Maintain the chronological order, and develop the story using all the senses

The first, most straightforward way to build your script is to keep the order we have just looked at and to simply work on the transitions between sections. Use the senses to describe different aspects of the story; what did it feel like to be in each part of the journey: the fear, the frustration, the sadness, the energy, the reluctance, the joy, the exhilaration.

(b) Just use pieces of the puzzle

A second way to build the script can be to select just a couple of key elements of the story. For example, one, life before, two, the call to action, and three, the action needed to move forward.

Consider this example:

During a story workshop, one of my participants said, "But I don't have this disaster of a life. My life is great. And anyway, how can any of this point to my business? I introduce people to fine, exquisite coffee. I am not saving anyone's life."

I asked her if she could remember life *without* her fine coffee, a life where the only coffee available was from a cheap vending machine in a dusty corner of the workplace.

I suggested she try a story like the following one.

"I've been a coffee drinker all my life, drinking buckets and buckets of tasteless, coloured water from a variety of vending machines in different corporate offices. But one day, everything changed. I bought coffee from a coffee cart in Copenhagen. In that moment, I discovered what real coffee was. True coffee that smelled like chocolate and tasted like liquid gold. I promptly realised my mission in life was to bring fine, quality coffee to the streets of Luxembourg."

Take a look at some of the other stories that I have included in the book where I talk about lessons learned. In these stories, I generally talk about what life is like before, what the wake-up call was, and what the way forward was. I might put them into different orders depending on the story.

(c) Start with the end in mind and work backward

A third way of building that script is to start with the end in mind: those lessons learned, the elixir, and the tools that you are bringing back after this journey. And then work backward to the, say, three key elements that got you to that place.

This sort of story might go something like this:

"As I look back over the last ten years since my first burnout, I can say that the biggest lesson I have learned is that the stories we tell ourselves are not necessarily the only truth that exists. When I learned to challenge those stories, I finally learned to make different choices that would build me up rather than tear me down. I want to tell you about how I have done that...."

EXPLAIN WHAT IT IS YOU DO IN A SIMPLE AND STRAIGHTFORWARD WAY

So, you have looked at introducing yourself to a client or audience to explain how you will add value, and you've thought about the case of telling your hero's journey to inspire an audience or how you have come through a particular trial.

In this third exercise, you will look at how you might explain what it is you do to someone you meet for the first time.

Here, we draw inspiration once again from the hero's journey, but this time you position yourself in a different way as the mentor or helper. This alternative approach recognises that our listeners are the heroes of their own journey, and they have their own dragons to slay. Our role is to help them slay the dragon by providing them with keys at critical points in their ongoing stories.

With this type of story, we demonstrate that we possess the tools critical to the hero's success.

Here is a basic structure for doing this:

"I help [insert type of client] to [do ... insert what it is you help them to do]. I do this by [insert how you help them to do this] and this allows them to [insert what this helps them to do].

If I were to tell this story in the context of the work I do with clients, I might say something like this.

"Good morning, everyone. My name is Joanna, and I am a public speaking coach.

"I help speakers who talk about very, very difficult subjects. They are passionate about their topic. They eat, live, and breathe it every day, but somewhere along the way forgot that mere mortals don't understand their work. When they get on stage, they struggle to translate their passion and subject into something understandable. Instead, they come across as boring and out of touch. They are then judged for their failings on stage rather than adored and respected for their game-changing ideas.

"I help them overcome this struggle by giving them the ability to see their subject matter through their audience's eyes. When they use that ability, they unlock the story within the technical data and connect with their audience on a deeper level. Now, instead of failing on stage, they succeed. They develop a voice that lets their ideas be heard."

To build your own mentor/hero story, explain the hero's situation and what they struggle with. Then, talk about what keys you provide and how they benefit the hero.

To craft your own mentor story, you may find one of the following outlines a good place to start.

"A company/ person was stuck with this problem _____, which meant _____. I provided them with _____ which enabled them to do _____."

Or

177

"The work I did with _____ enabled them to _____."

> ***Or***

"Today you are stuck with _____. This means that _____. My work will help you unlock _____."

REMEMBER "SO WHAT"

Throughout this chapter, one theme repeated itself: So what?

This question opens all sorts of doors. For example, it helps us spell out how our skills and achievements are of use to our clients, teams, and bosses. It also puts us in our listeners' shoes.

Shifting our perspectives in this way is critical. It helps us speak in a way people understand. It also makes people feel welcomed and heard. When they hear you speak, they don't think you're a show-off tooting your own horn. They hear someone who sympathizes with their plight and can help them overcome it.

Now, your ability to empathize and tell compelling stories won't happen overnight. Both take time, practice, and patience.

So, think about this chapter. What insights did you get about your story? And, what do you need to do next to author that story?

- To do today?

- To do next week?

- To do next month?

Finally, what resources do you need to bring your story to life and to the stage?

CONNECT

S omeone[92] once said, "Everybody is a genius. But if you judge a fish by its ability to climb a tree, it will live its whole life believing that it is stupid."

Guess what, fish get asked to climb trees every day. And if they don't manage it, they're made to believe they are stupid.

Let me give you a specific fish scenario. For the last twenty years, I've worked alongside brilliant people who have game-changing ideas about very difficult subjects. More often than not, they are asked to share their ideas with an audience at a conference, team meeting, or client event.

Some of them are hugely successful. Their energy and passion excite and inspire listeners.

But others struggle to translate their ideas into something accessible. When they get on stage, they are fish trying to climb trees. They don't know how to talk about their subject in a way that inspires the audience.

Instead, they face a sea of blank faces. The audience plays with their phones, looks out the window, or talks with their neighbours and never hears the speaker's ideas or sees the speaker's awesomeness. Rather, they judge the speaker for their failings on stage. The speaker is seen as dull, out of touch, and irrelevant.

These speakers get off the stage and flee back to the stacks of books or computer screen. Fundamentally, they don't enjoy being in the spotlight, particularly on stage and in front of a tough crowd. On top of that, they speak about a subject that is really hard to explain. They figure that no matter what they do, the audience is never going to grasp the subject matter, so why even bother?

But is it really just a question of the audience being too tough or the subject too hard? Or is that a cop-out?

92. This quote is often attributed to Einstein, but there is a doubt about whether it is the case.

And, what if the issue isn't the audience or the topic but the speaker's lack of tools to connect with the audience? That question changes the dynamic entirely, doesn't it?

I certainly think it does, so it pains me to see brilliant people judged and not heard because of poor presentation skills. And it hurts me to see brilliant people settle for such a situation. Because, you see, they don't have to settle. They have a choice. They can let the audience dictate how they are perceived, or they can choose to learn some skills that help them overcome communication barriers and connect with their audiences.

WHAT WILL YOU CHOOSE?

Because let's face it. The more you advance in your career, and the more you become known for your technical skill, the more you will be called upon, at some point, to talk about your subject matter.

Rather than dreading that call, embrace it. You love your subject. If you didn't, you wouldn't be working in the field you are. It's time for your audience to love your subject as much as you do, too.

I am convinced you can make any subject interesting to any audience with a few key steps. And I want to share these steps with you in this chapter. The chapter's straightforward exercises will encourage you to own your expertise and translate that technical knowledge into a compelling story that resonates with any audience.

Use the steps, and you'll be ready for the call to present. More importantly, your brilliant ideas and life-changing solutions won't be overlooked at the next conference, event, or meeting. You will connect with your audience and make an impact on them, not be judged as a fish flopping on stage.

TALK ABOUT YOUR TECHNICAL WORK IN A WAY MORTALS CAN UNDERSTAND

L et's do a reality check here. It is not your audience's responsibility to know or understand your world when you step onto the stage. It is your responsibility to understand theirs.

You are responsible to make the first move. Step into their world and see the subject through their eyes so that you can guide them through it.

If you learn how to do this, you'll take your life and career up a notch. Now, you're not only a technical genius. You're a person who can talk about your topic in a way that mere mortals can understand, and in a way that they can apply to their own lives.

This matters because you're not always talking with peers who have the same level of expertise as you. You could, more likely, be speaking with a person who is in the same field but with less experience, or to audiences who have no knowledge of your technical field.

Your translation abilities matter in other contexts, too. What if you were asked to write about your work in an article or blog? Could you do it without falling into jargon? And, could you do it in a way that brings the subject to life through stories that resonate with the reader?

Or maybe you're in a client meeting. Are you going to be able to discuss changes in your technical field and their impacts in a way the clients will understand? They don't care about the clauses in the law or the names of the case law—they want to know how what you're saying translates to their day-to-day life. What will they have to do in response to the changes you're talking about? Can you take the technical details of your field and turn them into pragmatic applications?

If you can, you'll see a spark in your listeners' eyes. They'll be engaged and listening to what you have to say. They'll also begin to see you as an expert in your field, which can cause them to want to work with you or influence them to pursue a new career path or mind-set.

LEARN TO SPEAK LIKE A HUMAN

You've probably spoken about your technical work in team meetings, trainings, or conversations with clients.[93] That means you already have an idea of what it is like to talk about a subject to non-experts. You also possess some indicators from the audience as to how good a job you have done in communicating your expertise. Let's assess how you're doing with speaking like a human so that you can build on existing strengths and skill sets.

1. Define what you want to achieve

What do you want to achieve when it comes to connecting with your audience? What are your goals?

For example, you might want to position yourself as an expert in the field by demonstrating the practical application of the technical work. Or you might want the audience to take an action or change a behaviour in light of new developments in your world.

---

93. And if you are a recent graduate and only just starting out in your career, let's face it, the chances are you have been presenting your work all the way through uni.

2. Discover your existing strengths

Where do you excel with talking about your technical work? What feedback have you received that indicates a successful connection with the audience?

3. Dream about possibilities

Let your imagination run wild. What could happen if you built your capacity for connection? What is the most unimaginable outcome possible?

4. Design Your roadmap

Look at the strengths you've identified. How can you use them to move forward, and to where?

5. Deliver on destiny

What steps do you need to take today to set your roadmap in motion?

Once you complete your roadmap and next steps, add some of the subsequent exercises into the mix. They'll help you forge stronger connections with the audience as you talk about your technical work.

PRACTICE: CONNECT IN
FIVE MINUTES

I t's great to be asked to share your knowledge and expertise. But where are you going to find the time to prepare for a talk in the midst of an already hectic workload?

If that's you, and you only have five minutes to take your talk from good to great, spend them getting clarity on the following question.

What is the one key message and takeaway of your talk? More specifically, if the audience walks out of the door remembering only a single thing, what must it be?

Now, make sure that single thing pervades the introduction, body, and conclusion of your speech, lecture, or presentation.[94]

---

94. If you aren't sure how to incorporate your *one* message, don't worry. That's why we have more exercises to complete in this chapter.

PRACTICE: FORM DEEPER, LONG-LASTING CONNECTIONS

To date, you've relied on technical genius. It's opened some doors, getting you asked to speak at conferences and meetings with other experts in your field or to give trainings to your teams.

These conversations leave you relatively at ease. It's simple to talk about your technical work with people who are as knowledgeable and passionate about it as you.

But things are starting to change. You are being asked to talk about your field of study with people who aren't familiar with who you are or what you do. They, however, need to know what you know.

Let's say, for instance, you are an expert in data privacy and the General Data Protection Regulation (GDPR). You know a lot about the subject. You also know your information affects every industry sector, so you want to position yourself as an expert. If you do, you'll attract clients from finance, e-commerce, and banking—*big* clients, in other words.

But they know nothing about data privacy. How are you going to convey the sense of urgency you feel about things? It's not as though you can just stand up and give the same speech you would to experts. If you do, you will lose your audience and, potentially, the deal.

That means it's time to translate your mass of technical information and knowledge into something mere mortals can understand. And you will with the exercises found in this chapter. They're simple techniques for the most past, but they will grab your audience's attention. They will also help you speak about your subject in a way that resonates with listeners and compels them to act.

In these exercises you will:

- Learn how to see your subject through the eyes of the audience

- Find examples to illustrate your key points

- Develop visual aids that complement, not drive, your talk

Believe me, the techniques work.[95] I know because I've seen good public speaking skills inspire people to change.

---

95. As with all good endeavours, they'll also take time. Put it in the time! It will pay off, turning you into a speaker who can interact with any audience, regardless of their technical know-how.

STEP INTO YOUR
AUDIENCE'S SHOES

Your talks are never about you and how fabulous you are. Nor are they about how much you know about some technical subject. Talks are first about your audience and, second, about how you can communicate your passion and game-changing ideas with them.

The concept might feel a little off-putting. But if you truly want to connect with your audience on a deeper level, you are going to have to shift your mind-set, step out of your shoes and speaker bubble, and step into your audience's shoes and world. The shoes might pinch. You could hobble for a bit. But if you want to get people on board with your ideas, embrace the discomfort and pain.

Step 1. Think about your audience

Because no two talks or audiences are the same, the first thing you need to do before working on your presentation is think about your audience. If you are talking about new accounting standards with accountants, you will present the story to them one way, and you will change your content as you walk into the next meeting with the IT team. Accountants want to talk about what they need to change in the accounting treatment of particular elements; the IT team cares about how to implement the standards in the company's accounting software.

Learning to think that the most important thing about your talk is the audience is important because:

- It focuses on the audience's level of expertise, helping you avoid jargon and teaching you to speak in the audience's language

- It helps you understand the world your audience lives in, which can guide you toward relevant examples and analogies

- It identifies unspoken questions or concerns the audience may have about you, giving you time to decide how to answer them either during or after your speech

The next few questions will help you determine a potential audience's expertise, outlook, and questions. Take about ten minutes to go through them. Write down your thoughts so that you have something to refer back to.[96]

- Who will be in the audience? What are their roles, backgrounds, and experiences with the subject matter? What expectations or preconceptions do they have about you, the speaker, or your presentation?

- What's important to them? What do they need to know? What problem are they trying to solve? What are things they hold dear?

---

96. You will see some overlaps with the previous chapter on story, and that is deliberate. The chapter on story looked at what elements of your story were important for your audience. The questions in this chapter are about finding simple ways to talk about your technical work. These elements may be the same, but they are more likely to be different.

- What questions are they likely to have about you or the topic? Remember that these questions may be voiced or silent—the elephant in the room.[97]

If your audience is going to be anything larger than a small group,[98] you likely won't be able to get specific about each person. But you can still think in terms of demographics, subgroups, age, gender, and other details to create a picture of your audience and their collective concerns.

Step 2. Define your purpose behind talking about this subject

It's nearly time to think about the subject in detail, and I get it, there is a lot you want to talk about with this topic. You've already waited to start writing your speech because I told you to think about your audience first. But it's still not time to jump into the details of your subject.

First, answer this question.

Why do you want to talk about this topic?

Go on, tell me. What was your first reaction when I asked, "Why do you want to talk about this topic?"

---

97. Sometimes, the questions might be typical and come up about the technical aspects of your work every time you talk about it. For example, you have already given a few talks on the subject, and every single time, the same question pops up. The questions might also be about the implications and may remain unasked. For example, if you talk about the automation of audit function or tax returns, the audience may be concerned about job security. Will they lose their job to data analytics and artificial intelligence? The audience might never feel comfortable enough to ask the question out loud, but it will be at the forefront of their minds for the duration of your talk. That is what I mean by the elephant in the room—the unasked question that deafens in its silence.

98. Okay, so what's a small group and what's a large group? Think in terms of anything up to about seven or eight people as a small group. It's an arbitrary figure, I must admit, but it will give you a starting point.

Was it, "My boss asked me to"? Maybe you thought, "Well, it's a conference on new legislation. We need to be seen there," or maybe it was, "I want to be visible in the marketplace, that's why."

Okay, okay, I get it. Those are common, and legitimate, reasons. But they're surface level. Dig deeper into your reason(s) for giving a talk. Do this by asking:

What do you want the audience to do, think, or feel as a result of your talk?

Maybe you want the audience to act by changing how they record expenses in their books. Then again, maybe you want them to think about something differently, such as the GDPR[99]. A successful talk might be one in which they view the regulations differently and implement the rules well in advance of the deadline.

Perhaps your goal is to shift a perspective or perception. You want the audience to change how they view an application like artificial intelligence, learning to see it as an opportunity for all rather than as a threat to job security.

Maybe you want the audience to view you as an expert, with the experience and credibility needed to provide them with the best service. Or perhaps you want them to get excited about the opportunities available as a result of new developments in your field. Because of your talk, they will see you as uniquely equipped to help them maximise those prospects.

Do you see how those answers differ from "I want to be more visible"?

I always recommend digging for clarity when it comes to your "why" because it gives you a "red line" that brings your

---

99. I have used the data protection regulations as an example as they were a big talking point in 2018. However, there are new regulations and developments in all sorts of fields every year. Chances are, you will talk about them at some point.

talk together. Knowing the "why" also enables you to place relevant sign posts throughout the talk to make sure you guide your audience to where you want them to go.

The "why" helps you connect with your audience on a deeper level, too, because:

- The "why" is personal, even if it's a combination of personal and professional elements

- It keeps your ideas simple and precise

- It helps you come across as organised and consistent, which reinforces your credibility and strengthens your connection with the audience

So, to summarise, spend another ten or so minutes asking yourself the question "What is it that I want this audience to do, think, or feel as a result of what I say about the topic?" Try to articulate your answer in fewer than fifteen words.

Step 3. Define what you want to talk about

Finally. Let's talk about the subject of your speech.

As you think about your topic, spend about ten minutes jotting down a bullet list of things you would like to cover in your speech.

This is a brain dump exercise designed to get your thoughts all out there. Afterward, we'll come back and select things to cover and things to leave out.

Bring It All Together

All done? Great. Now that you've done all that, find the key in the sweet spot: the overlap. Look for where your audience, your why, and your topic come together.

Think about the three as though they were a Venn diagram.

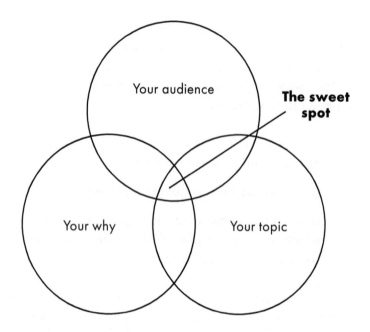

Identifying the overlap/sweet spot is essential because:

- It allows you to position your key message from the perspective of the audience

- It identifies material you must absolutely include in your talk, as well as elements superfluous for this audience

- It articulates the benefits of your presentation to the audience right from the start

So, take the notes you wrote for steps 1, 2 and 3, and answer these questions. This part of the exercise should take thirty minutes, tops.

- Where is the overlap between all three elements? What is the key message or takeaway that will tap into all the elements?

- What's in it for the audience? How will they benefit tangibly by listening to you speak about this subject? To think about this, look at the things that are important to them and how your subject relates to those things.

  For example, imagine you are talking about Excel formulae to a room of new graduates coming to work for the firm. Your talk will get them up to speed and hit the ground running when they start their first audit jobs. They will be able to save time because they already know what formulae to use. And, a huge plus, they won't look stupid in front of their bosses.

- What things must you absolutely include in your talk? What can you leave out?

  To do this, review the things you wrote down in your bullet list about the topic. As you go through the list, identify which points must be included in light of your audience and your "why."

  One thing in particular to think about are the questions your audience might have—which will you answer in your talk, and which will you wait to answer should someone raise the point directly?

- What other insights come to you as you look at the three steps and the places where they overlap?

Wowzah!! That was a lot of work, I know. But if you construct a Venn diagram, you will:

- Identify what's important to your audience.

- Get clear on your topic and the "why" behind it.

- Identify where your passion and the audience's interests overlap.

So, as you proceed to prepare your presentation, let the above questions act as beacons.

- Use them to structure your talk and identify examples that help your audience relate to the subject.

- Think about these elements as you rehearse your talk, remembering to speak in your audience's language, not your field's technical jargon.

- Recall the benefits to the audience and place clear signposts throughout your talk to get the audience where you want them to go.

Above all, use the questions and steps to keep yourself in your audience's shoes. Doing so helps you explain your subject simply. It also creates a connection with the audience so that they care about your subject. And when they care, the magic begins. You'll witness an audience excited and inspired to act even as you become the kind of speaker you've only ever dreamed of.

USE STORIES TO REDUCE COMPLEXITY

We've talked about your audience and started you thinking about your subject through their eyes. Now, to connect with the audience, we need to build on the subject through stories and examples.

"Wait!" I hear you cry, "Stories? I'm not telling fairy tales to my audience. I'm no Hans Christian Andersen or J. K. Rowling.

"I'm an *intellectual*. I talk about serious things like taxes, artificial intelligence, and cybersecurity. There's no place for stories there. It's all about the facts…right?"

Hang on. Facts tell but stories sell. And in this case, stories will help you "sell" your ideas without becoming "salesy" or losing your audience with the "blah blah."[100] They'll also demonstrate you know what you are talking about, establishing your credibility and authority.

If you're reading this chapter, I imagine you want those things. You wish to position yourself as an expert in your field and convince the audience you can help them in their business. So, I'm going to let you in on a little secret. When you

---

100. You know what "blah blah" is. It's the hot air that fills the gap in, oh, so many pseudo-intellectual talks.

vomit a bunch of facts or recite legislation at your audience, the audience does not think, "Oh, (s)he knows her subject."

Rather, they often doubt your knowledge and expertise. If the audience doesn't understand anything you are talking about, they will simply conclude you know how to copy and paste the legislation. You don't, however, know how it works. Worse, they question your ability to help them implement change, legislation-related or otherwise.

Stories, though, make a difference. They apply the facts to real-world situations, letting the audience see how the subject relates to their lives. Stories also grow the audience's confidence in your ability to help them take forward steps with their lives, careers, and businesses.

Here are three ways to use stories in your technical talks, followed by a couple of exercises to find relevant and personal stories.

METHOD 1. USE STORIES TO ESTABLISH CREDIBILITY

When we meet someone for the first time, we quickly decide whether we like the person and whether they are any good at what they do. The same thing is at work when the audience "meets" you as a speaker for the first time.

So, when you speak in public, part of your task is to establish credibility—getting a placement on the stage or panel isn't enough to instil confidence. If the audience doesn't believe you can bring them value, they are going to switch off early on.[101] Because of that, you have to show you know how the topic impacts the audience on a day-to-day basis as well as illustrate how you can help them navigate the subject.

---

101. How often have you found yourself switching off a speaker shortly after they begin to speak, irrespective of the glowing introduction given by the Master of Ceremonies, simply because they do not come across as *credible*?

Stories about how you have dealt with the topic and examples of how other businesses do the same are great ways to accomplish both goals. Stories demonstrate you understand how the topic applies to the audience's businesses and lives. They also showcase how you can help people in the audience without resorting to a recitation of your CV.

METHOD 2. USE STORIES TO EXPLAIN DIFFICULT BITS

Repeat after me: "My audience is intelligent. They just aren't experts in the same field as me."

All that means is that you're probably going to come across some difficult bits in your talk that will require explanation.

One way to break down the difficult pieces is through stories and analogies.

For example, one of my clients was talking about artificial intelligence. She wanted to explain how a computer enabled with AI learns as compared to a human. She backed up the idea with her "why." She said people often believe artificial intelligence means computers learn and compute vast sums of data in the same way but faster than humans do. This belief instils fear in grown men and women throughout the world; they think computers are going to take over their jobs and they will no longer have any value. But, she explained, computers *don't* learn the same way as humans. Plus, AI doesn't need to be scary. Humans will always have a place in the world.

To explain the differences between how machines and humans learn, I suggested my client have the audience imagine they had to bake and decorate a chocolate cake for the Royal Wedding. In the first instance, the audience listed all the things they would do themselves. They would look up a recipe on the internet, ask their grandmother for tips, and watch one or two videos on how to decorate a wedding cake.

Then, my client created a second instance. She went line by line comparing the computer's actions to the audience's. Doing so showed that rather than viewing two or three videos on YouTube, the computer might watch at least one hundred. In addition, it might sift through *thousands* of recipes.

However, the computer would not be able to determine which recipe was the best one for the Royal Wedding although it might be able to take an average of all of them[102]. And, if the recipe asked for chocolate to be used, the computer would not necessarily know what chocolate was. It would have to look up additional information before being able to proceed.

METHOD 3. USE STORIES TO ILLUSTRATE WORST AND BEST-CASE SCENARIOS

As a generic guideline, the majority of your talks will probably help people do things like save money, make money, build reputations, be more efficient, or establish their brands. And, on the contrary, there be warnings to be told of how if the audience doesn't follow your guidance, things can go horribly wrong.

So, depending on the speech in question, give them examples of when those events have happened to your clients. Show the best of cases and the worst of cases.[103] Bring reality home so that they can *see* what will happen if they act—or don't.

None of this is rocket science. When you remember your audience is made up of human beings who want to connect and learn, and let go of the idea that you need to prove your

---

102. Imagine for a moment what an average recipe would be. Say you had a five-star recipe that used three eggs, another that used four, and a third that called for no eggs. The average of the three recipes is 2.33 eggs. Do you want to work out how to measure 2.33 eggs? Probably not; it's a ridiculous suggestion.

103. Dickens was no fool. He knew that best and worst-case scenarios intrigued readers. The same notion applies to listeners.

intelligence with facts and figures, you're free to bring your facts and figures to life with all kinds of stories.[104]

The question is, where are those stories and how do you find them? I'm glad you asked because we're going to get concrete and find some examples and stories for your speeches.

Step 1. Identify three key points to guide the audience to the key takeaway

In the previous exercises, you stepped into your audience's shoes, you thought about your why, and you thought about your topic. Then, you looked for the overlap, the place where the audience's hopes and your intentions intersect so you can come up with the key takeaway and message for the audience.

Return to the Venn diagram portion of the exercise. Now ask, "What three points would guide my listeners to the key message or takeaway?" Write your answers in the first column or on a separate piece of paper.

Key takeaway of your talk: _____

Key Point	Type of Story	Specific Story
1.		
2.		
3.		

---

104. Funny stories work, too. Laughter can get a point across a whole lot better than a stuffy, stilted story. However, the story must always have a point. If you put stories in for the sake of being funny, you risk losing overall impact.

Step 2. Identify the kind of stories you need to tell

In light of your three main points, what kinds of stories do you need to use and to what end?

For example:

- Stories to establish your credibility as an expert?

- Stories to explain the hard bits?

- Stories to demonstrate the benefits of a particular course of action?

- Stories to bring home pain points or horror stories of not taking a particular course of action?

Key takeaway of your talk: _____

Key Point	Type of Story	Specific Story
1.		
2.		
3.		

You may have one or two types of stories for each point. Write them all down. You'll figure out the best story type and its specifics in the next step.

Step 3. Choose the stories you want to use

As you look at each key point and the kind of story needed to illustrate it, identify particular examples. These should be from your own experiences, personal or professional, or examples from your clients. Jot a brief note in the third column.

Key takeaway of your talk:

Key Point	Type of Story	Specific Story
1.		
2.		
3.		

Step 4. Determine the details

With the stories identified, decide how much detail you will give and start writing the key elements of the story.

For example, you can tell the story from a high-level view: "We had a client who was stuck with … and we were able to help them …" This angle has the advantage of getting straight to the point and giving a concise and precise problem and resolution.

Alternatively, you might want to go into more detail. Set out:

- The situation before the problem
- What happened to make the client take action
- The action required
- The result

The second story type involves more detail and requires more practice. However, it has the benefit of sweeping your audience into the story.

Whichever way you choose, mark at least two pieces: (1) the key pieces of the story and (2) the learning point or conclusion to the story. The key points you wrote earlier will help with that, guiding you toward plot points and conclusions that link to the overall message of your talk.

Key takeaway of your talk: _____

Key Point	Type of Story	Specific Story
1.		
2.		
3.		

Step 5. Practice telling the story

Finally, once you have drafted the key elements of the different stories, practice telling them. Practice helps you assess timing and avoid wandering off into tangents. Practice at home in front of your mirror. You can also record yourself. If you do, follow the recording by carefully listening to the audio. Doing so will point out the places where you wobble or where things are unclear.

By now, you have done a lot of work. You've established a skeleton for your talk and identified elements for your introduction, body, and conclusion. Next, we'll cover visual aids. They're important to cementing your message in people's minds. But spoiler alert: Slides are not your only option.

COMPLEMENT WITH SLIDES

How much do you really think about the slides you present in your talks?

According to Mayer's multimedia principle[xxxviii], if you want to explain difficult concepts, you should present them not only verbally but also visually. In other words: Give your audience something to look at, not just to listen to.

This idea hardly comes as a surprise, especially if you work in a technical field. You might not know the name of the learning theory, but you certainly know and have used the idea, preparing hundreds, if not thousands, of slides over the course of your career.

Which is awesome.

But something about our slides isn't quite as awesome: our misconceptions. Over the years, I've built and seen many, many slides in all sorts of different contexts. Those years and experience have let me identify a few common misconceptions that can affect our approach to slides and cost us our connection with the audience.

So, let's talk about them. Once the misconceptions are out of the way, we'll work through a couple of exercises to make sure our slides work for, instead of against, us.

MISCONCEPTION 1. SLIDES BEFORE STORY

How many times have you said to yourself, "Right, I have a technical presentation coming up. I should prepare my slides."

It seems like a practical thing to do—getting the slides down first and thinking about the story later. Creating the visual elements puts something tangible on the screen. However, I believe this approach is back to front. What often happens with it, particularly when the speaker has highly technical content, is:

- Slides become incredibly complex, technical, and over-loaded with information

- Speakers cling to the deck for dear life because the slides, not the story, dictate the talk

On the other hand, when a story drives the talk, it is easier for the speaker to stop worrying about the slides and start enjoying the story they're telling. And when that transpires, strong connections with the audience occur.

> **Fact.** If you really want to connect with your audience, work on the story first and the slides second. Tell the audience a story they can relate to and then reinforce it with visual aids—images, props, slides, whatever it takes.

MISCONCEPTION 2. MORE WORDS EQUALS GREATER INTELLIGENCE

I used to be a tax consultant who regularly talked about VAT, on and off the stage. It's a highly complex and difficult topic with multifaceted aspects.

In the early days, I was still figuring out the difficult bits for myself—it is impossible to be the expert on every single aspect of the field.[105] My lack of knowledge showed: Whenever I talked about the difficult bits I didn't understand, I vomited the legislation onto a slide and hoped for the best.

You see, I believed that the more words I put on the slide the more intelligent I would appear to the audience. They would be convinced I knew what I was talking about! But that's not what happened at all.

As I think about the hundreds of technical slides I have seen over the years, I can only conclude other speakers have also believed the number of words on the screen corresponds to how smart the audience thinks they are. But once again we need a reality check.

When an audience sees a bunch of words on the slides, all they think is "Oh, crikey, another boring overcharged slide. Do they really expect me to read this? Where's my iPhone? Time to check my emails."

The audience checks out because they're perfectly capable of reading your slides on their own time. They don't need you to read to them. They do need, however, your unique perspective on the information.

So, change your approach to your slides. Speak about your key ideas and use slides to heighten the audience's understanding of the ideas. If you do, the audience will pay attention to you, not scroll through emails or Instagram.

How can you do this effectively? Here are five things you might want to think about:

- Limit the number of words on the slide[106]

- Write in bullet points rather than full sentences

---

105. The VAT treatment of payment vouchers. Please don't ask me to go there. ☺

106. Advice on the actual number varies depending on who you talk to, and I have seen guidance from as few as six words to as many as thirty-six.

- Use images[107] where appropriate[108]

- Be consistent in the font size throughout your slides; avoid anything smaller than 18–20 points

- Be conscious of the colours you use on the slides—black, dark blue, and red are effective colours because they can be seen from a distance, while colours like yellow are difficult[109]

Fact. We can't really believe the audience likes to see words upon words on the screen, can we? No. Use your slides to illustrate rather than regurgitate.

MISCONCEPTION 3. SLIDES ARE THE ONLY ACCEPTABLE VISUAL AIDS

Somehow, we've been indoctrinated with the idea that slides are the only acceptable visual aid. They're not. We have other possibilities, such as:

---

107. When using images, think about aspects like copyright and user rights. Your organisation might also have restrictions as to what images you can use, and in what circumstances (e.g. there might be a set of pre-approved images to use, or you might be able to use freely available stock photos). Learn these requirements before preparing your slides.

108. A small warning about images. A picture paints a thousand words when they are appropriate. Imagery for the sake of imagery doesn't do anything. Your touchstone should be that if you explain things well, the image should speak for itself.

109. Depending on where you work or where you are speaking, there may also be certain branding guidelines about the font, the size, and the colours. Do you know what these requirements are? If not, how might you be able to find them out?

- Objects[110]

- Flip charts,

- Videos

- Blackboard

- Hand-outs

- Games

- Banners

- Posters

- Tablet computers

My personal favourite, as a complement to your slides, is the one-page hand-out. This hand-out doesn't have all the slides on it. Rather, it's a single A4-size document that sets out the key points of your talk. These key elements might prompt the audience to write notes—increasing engagement and interactivity—or they may simply summarize the key takeaways. Whatever option you choose, this single-page document is important. It gives the audience something concrete to take home with them and refer back to.

A one-pager may not work for your audience. That's fine. Your choice of visual aid should always be informed by where and with whom you are speaking. But I would hope your choice would not be restricted to "but the audience expects slides." Defeat expectations! You'll leave a memorable impression.

Fact. Slides may be the norm, but they aren't the be-all and end-all. Use the visual aid that best expresses your story and key takeaway.

---

110. It's like Show and Tell from when you were at primary school. Use a yo-yo, a watch, a set of tennis balls—whatever works to get your main idea across.

211

As you head off and prepare for your next talk, I ask you to think twice about the slides you prepare. Remember the basic premise we are working on: Slides and other visual aids should complement what you are saying. They should not make your subject more difficult to understand. ☺

To shift your approach to slides and visual aids, I recommend using the following three steps. They've helped me find new ways to explain complex topics, leading to stronger connections with my audience.

Step 1. Define your key message and story
What is the story you want to convey with your talk? Recall it by looking at the other exercises from this chapter.

Step 2: Choose the appropriate visual aid
What visual aids best complement your message? Is it the age-old favourite (slides) or something else?

Step 3: Optimise the visual content
How can you optimise your visual aids to keep matters simple rather than over-complicate them? Run a litmus test. Show your visual aids to a friend and test whether they understand the concepts easily.

KEEP THINGS SIMPLE

This chapter focused on getting into your audience's shoes so that you can better connect with people. After all, you won't always be speaking with peers and experts in your field. Even if you are conversing with well-seasoned colleagues, surely they would also like a break from the jargon.

Offer them one by focusing on simple ideas—key messages or takeaways—and stories. If nothing else, the streamlined format will allow people to follow along and act on your message. And stories make you relatable. Now, people, including your peers, view you as someone who not only knows their stuff but can also apply it to real-world situations.

Also, remember to use visual aids to enhance your presentation. The visuals are not replacements for a story, nor are they an excuse to vomit words on the screen. They are there to support your words, to create an image that the listener remembers days, weeks, and months after the lecture or presentation.

Keeping all that in mind, what are some insights you've gained from this chapter for talking about your work?

Now, what are your next steps when it comes to connecting with your audience?

- To do today?

- To do next week?

- To do next month?

Finally, what resources do you need to implement your plans?

CHOICE

It's 5 p.m. on the afternoon of my 45th birthday. I finished work about a week ago for Christmas. I am enjoying some time at home in Belfast, having a real break.

It's 5 p.m. on the afternoon of my 45th birthday. I am eating cake and sitting with my parents and sister for a Dentons' day out. The waitress just brought our afternoon tea, a birthday present from mum and dad.

It's 5 p.m. on my 45th birthday, and I have finally learned I don't have to choose between health and success, work and family. I can have both.

In the past ten years, everything has changed in my life. I no longer work as a tax consultant. After my second burnout in 2014, I moved out of consulting and into an in-house role where I helped colleagues prepare for speaking at conferences or pitching to clients. Two years later, I left corporate life completely. I started a business doing what I love—helping clients get their lives back, both on and off stage.

But have I learned to balance work and life, health and success?

Well, I am getting there.[111]

I no longer work for weeks and months on end. But putting two full days of work into every 24-hour period, combined with 40 years of high achieving, doesn't disappear overnight. The habits and attitudes I learned as a child and an adult linger. Because of that, I still have some things to learn, such as not over-committing myself in my diary. I am also working on not trying to please everyone at the detriment of my health.

Even then, my inner critic still comes calling every single day because I am pushing myself outside my comfort zone. But where it would have paralyzed me before, I now manage it. When my stomach starts to churn and my palms get sweaty, I put on my "big girl" pants and embrace the discomfort.

---

111. Perhaps that'll be my new mantra: "I am getting there." We're all works in progress.

I guess I have learned some things along the way. Besides being able to handle my inner critic, I now know I am worth looking after. Four years of reiki and relaxation (and a whole lot of chocolate) have also taught me I am the one person who not only knows what my body needs but can also listen and respond to it.

I also know what I am capable of. Leaving corporate life to start my own business, despite all the uncertainty, has shown me that. Like building office furniture—I no longer have a building services department or furniture fairy, so it's just me, myself, and I. I can sort out IT problems[112] while organising successful workshops month after month, too.

If I regret anything, it's that I didn't know back then what I know now. My life and career would have been very different if I had understood I didn't have to choose between success and health. I could have both.

But then, hindsight is always 20/20. Plus, if I hadn't had my burnouts, I might never have looked for a different way I to live. I did, though, and it's made all the difference. It's led me to where I am now, doing what I do, and making a difference in the lives of my clients.

This is what I wish for you today after reading this book.

It's to take back control of your truths and make better choices.

I wrote this book to flag a number of stories and truths that we tell ourselves. We might think that those truths are helping us, but they actually lead us down the road to bad choices or cases where we don't actually choose at all. What I have tried to do is shine a light on these stories so you can challenge them. So that you can make up your own mind about whether they are helping or hindering you. If they are helping, Godspeed, and keep doing what you are doing. But if, in the cold light of day, these truths are hindering you,

---

112. Yep, "Turn it off; turn it on again," really does work.

how could you change those narratives and stories and make different choices? The first step will always be awareness of the stories in the first place. I hope that by now you can start to see them. I also hope that you have some ideas about changing those stories and moving forward, concrete exercises that can take your forward into the next chapter of your life.

I invite you to notice the choices you are making, and the ones you are not making, and find the story behind it.

What would it be like if you started to choose yourself and change your story?

Today is the first day of the rest of your life. Your future is waiting for you, ready for the taking. All you have to do is choose it.

What future, full of joy and colour and love and laughter, will you choose today?

ACKNOWLEDGEMENTS

You know what, writing a book is bloody hard, and over the last eighteen months, a lot of people have put up with my gurning and whinging and enthusing and crying—all in different doses. I want to say thank you to many of them in particular.

Thank you to Charlie Gilkey, who sent me away in early 2018 for a week and told me to "write and see what happens." Slowly, what was meant to be a PDF with some free content became tens of thousands of words, but I wouldn't have even thought it possible if he hadn't nudged me in the right direction to start with.

Thanks, too, to my editors Erin Feldman at Write Right Words and Chris O'Byrne and his team at JETLAUNCH. The right doses of kicking my ass and helping me to manage my inner fears as they came up time and time again meant that I got through this more or less in one piece.

Thank you to those who read early copies of the book to give feedback—Renee Aakrann, Sylvie Maestri, Emeline Baud, Andreea Flintoaca, and Jessica Whytehorne—and to those who read and gave precious additional input on specific excerpts, Jonathan Fields, Tara Mohr, Gretchen Remners, and Kimberley Belle. Thank you for taking the time to do this and provide such valuable input. Thank you to Renee Morel and Annie Ricci and Katherine North who regularly put up with me going on about the book month after month, even when it didn't seem to me to be going anywhere too fast, and have never once said, "Is it not bloody finished, yet?"

Thank you to the TedX teams of both IMT Atlantique and the University of Surrey who gave me a stage to tell my story and really hone the details, and to all those behind the scenes helping me prepare. Thank you to the team of Sofitel Grand Ducal in Luxembourg who looked after me so well when I moved in for ten days to write during a bonkers heatwave in the summer of 2018. And thank you to the Luxembourg Powerhouses and The Infinity Alliance group who always had my back and were ready to send words of encouragement when I really needed them.

To everyone who supported me on my journey over the last ten years as I came back from my burnouts and changed my life. Thank you, in particular, to Leen Pattyn, who was at the end of the phone when I made that call in 2014, and to Aileen Hopper, who dragged me to my first ever hot yoga class about a week later.

And finally, to Mum, Dad, and Rowan, who are always there for me. No matter what. Thank you.

ENDNOTES

i.   Lyubomirsky, Sheldon, and Schkade. "Pursuing Happiness: The Architecture of Sustainable Change." *Review of General Psychology*. 9.2 (2005): 111–31.

ii.   Witvliet, Charlotte VanOyen, et al. "Gratitude Predicts Hope and Happiness: A Two-Study Assessment of Traits and States." *The Journal of Positive Psychology*. 15 Jan. 2018. 5 June 2018. https://www.tandfonline.com/doi/full/10.1080/17439760.2018.1424924

iii.   https://positivepsychology.com/benefits-of-gratitude/

iv.   Conversano, Ciro, et al. "Optimism and Its Impact on Mental and Physical Well-Being." *Clinical, Practical, Epidemiological Mental Health*. 6 (2010): 25–9. 12 June 2018. https://www.ncbi.nlm.nih.gov/pmc/articles/PMC2894461/

v.   Steinhilber, Brianna. "How to Train Your Brain to Be More Optimistic." *NBC News*. 24 Aug. 2017. 12 June 2018. https://www.nbcnews.com/better/health/how-train-your-brain-be-more-optimistic-ncna795231

vi.   Pappas, Stephanie. "Why Comparing Yourself to Others is Normal." *LiveScience*. 20 July 2016. 12 June 2018. https://www.livescience.com/55471-comparing-yourself-to-others-is-normal.html.

vii.   Becker, Joshua. "A Helpful Guide to Stop Comparing Yourself to Others." *becomingminimalist*. 12 June 2018. https://www.becomingminimalist.com/compare-less/.

viii.   Kindness.org. "7 Days of Intentional Kindness: Our First kindlab Study resulted in an Improved Outlook on Life." *Medium*. 17 Apr. 2017. 13 June 2018. https://medium.com/kindlab/7-days-of-intentional-kindness-9bac913155b4.

ix.   Zaki, Jamil. "Kindness Contagion." *Scientific American*. 26 July 2016. 13 June 2018. https://www.scientificamerican.com/article/kindness-contagion/.

x.   Mental Health Foundation. 5 June 2018. https://www.mentalhealth.org.uk/publications/relationships-21st-century-forgotten-foundation-mental-health-and-wellbeing

xi. Mayo Clinic Staff. "Forgiveness: Letting Go of Grudges and Bitterness." *Mayo Clinic*. 13 June 2018. https://www.mayoclinic.org/healthy-lifestyle/adult-health/in-depth/forgiveness/art-20047692.

xii. Czikszentmihalyi, Mihaly. *Flow: The Psychology of Optimal Experience* 1990; see also https://positivepsychology.com/mihaly-csikszentmihalyis-flow/

xiii. Bryant, Fred B. and Veroff, Joseph. *Savoring: A New Model of Positive Experience*. Psychology Press: London. 2006.

xiv. Latham, Gary P. "Goal-Setting Theory: Causal Relationships, Mediators, and Moderators." *Oxford Research*. May 2016. 13 June 2018. http://psychology.oxfordre.com/view/10.1093/acrefore/9780190236557.001.0001/acrefore-9780190236557-e-12#.

xv. https://www.prri.org/press-release/new-survey-one-five-americans-spiritual-not-religious/

xvi. Anxiety and Depression Association of America. "Understand the Facts: Physical Activity Reduces Stress." 13 June 2018. https://adaa.org/understanding-anxiety/related-illnesses/other-related-conditions/stress/physical-activity-reduces-st.

xvii. https://www.psychologytoday.com/us/blog/you-illuminated/201204/brain-scans-show-how-meditation-improves-mental-focus

xviii. VIA Institute on Character. Character Strengths Test. 16 May 2018. https://www.viacharacter.org/survey/account/register.

xix. Gallup. *CliftonStrengths*. 16 May 2018. https://www.gallupstrengthscenter.com/.

xx. Kreiman, Gabriel, et al. "Imagery Neurons in the Brain." Nature 408 (2000): 357–61. 24 July 2018.h https://www.nature.com/articles/35042575.

xxi. Dweck, Carol. *Mindset: The Psychology for Success*. New York: Ballantine, 2007.

xxii. Mineo, Liz. "Good Genes are Nice, But Joy is Better." *The Harvard Gazette*. 11 Apr. 2017. 05 Aug. 2018. https://news.harvard.edu/gazette/story/2017/04/over-nearly-80-years-harvard-study-has-been-showing-how-to-live-a-healthy-and-happy-life/.

xxiii. Baumeister, Roy, and Leary, Mark. "The Need to Belong: Desire for Interpersonal Attachments as a Fundamental Human Motivation." *Psychological Bulletin* 117 (3) (1995): 497–529. 05 Aug. 2018. http://psycnet.apa.org/record/1995-29052-001.

xxiv. Schawbel, Dan. "Brene Brown: Why Human Connection Will Bring Us Closer Together." Forbes. 12 Sept. 2017. 05 Aug. 2018. https://www.forbes.com/sites/danschawbel/2017/09/12/brene-brown-why-human-connection-will-bring-us-closer-together.

xxv. Brown, Brene. *Daring Greatly: How the Courage to Be Vulnerable Transforms the Way We live, Love, Parent, and Lead*. New York: Avery. 2012.

xxvi.   Brown, Brene *Rising Strong* Vermillion, London 2015

xxvii.   Gilman, Sarri. "Good Boundaries Free You." TedX Talks. 17 Dec. 2015. 8 Aug. 2018. https://www.youtube.com/watch?v=rtsHUeKnkC8.

xxviii. Brown, Brene. *The Gifts of Imperfection: Let Go of Who You Think You're Supposed to Be and Embrace Who You Are.* Center City: Hazelden. 2010.

xxix.   Covey, Stephen R. *The 7 Habits of Highly Effective People.* New York: Simon and Schuster. 2013

xxx.   Cuddy, Amy; Fiske, Susan; Glick, Peter. "Warmth and competence as Universal Dimensions of Social Perception: The stereotype content model and the BIAS map." https://www.sciencedirect.com/science/article/pii/S0065260107000020?via%3Dihub

xxxi.   Ross, Howard. "Exploring Unconscious Bias." CDO Insights 2:5 (2008). 5 Aug. 2018. http://www.cookross.com/docs/UnconsciousBias.pdf.

xxxii.   Project Implicit. https://implicit.harvard.edu/implicit/.

xxxiii. http://www.pnas.org/content/111/39/14027 for the research by Polly Wiessner

xxxiv.   TED talk by Uri Hasson on brain coupling https://www.ted.com/talks/uri_hasson_this_is_your_brain_on_communication

xxxv.   Campbell, Joseph. *The Hero with a thousand faces.* New World Library, Third edition, 2012

xxxvi.   Vogler, Chris. *The Writer's Journey: Mythic Structure for Writers.* Michael Wiese Productions: Studio City. 2007.

xxxvii. Duarte, Nancy. *Resonate: Present Visual Stories that Transform Audiences.* John Wiley and Sons: Hoboken. 2010.

xxxviii. Mayer, Richard. Multimedia Learning. Cambridge UP: London. 2009

Lightning Source UK Ltd.
Milton Keynes UK
UKHW020651011119
352675UK00002B/2/P

9 781641 841542